2018

12-MONTH DAILY PLANNER

BELLE CITY GIFTS

Belle City Gifts
Racine, Wisconsin, USA

Belle City Gifts is an imprint of BroadStreet Publishing Group LLC.
Broadstreetpublishing.com

For I Know the Plans
2018 Planner
© 2017 by BroadStreet Publishing

ISBN 978-1-4245-5506-2

Design by Garborg Design Works | garborgdesign.com
Compiled and edited by Michelle Winger | literallyprecise.com

Printed in China.

17   18   19   20   21   22   23   7   6   5   4   3   2   1

PERSONAL INFORMATION

Name _____

Address _____

_____

_____

_____

Phone   (h) _____

         (w) _____

         (c) _____

_____

Email addresses _____

_____

Emergency Contacts _____

_____

_____

_____

Family and Friends _____

_____

_____

_____

_____

_____

_____

_____

_____

_____

_____

2018 AT A GLANCE

JANUARY 2018

S	M	T	W	T	F	S
	1	2	3	4	5	6
7	8	9	10	11	12	13
14	15	16	17	18	19	20
21	22	23	24	25	26	27
28	29	30	31			

FEBRUARY 2018

S	M	T	W	T	F	S
				1	2	3
4	5	6	7	8	9	10
11	12	13	14	15	16	17
18	19	20	21	22	23	24
25	26	27	28			

MARCH 2018

S	M	T	W	T	F	S
				1	2	3
4	5	6	7	8	9	10
11	12	13	14	15	16	17
18	19	20	21	22	23	24
25	26	27	28	29	30	31

APRIL 2018

S	M	T	W	T	F	S
1	2	3	4	5	6	7
8	9	10	11	12	13	14
15	16	17	18	19	20	21
22	23	24	25	26	27	28
29	30					

MAY 2018

S	M	T	W	T	F	S
		1	2	3	4	5
6	7	8	9	10	11	12
13	14	15	16	17	18	19
20	21	22	23	24	25	26
27	28	29	30	31		

JUNE 2018

S	M	T	W	T	F	S
					1	2
3	4	5	6	7	8	9
10	11	12	13	14	15	16
17	18	19	20	21	22	23
24	25	26	27	28	29	30

JULY 2018

S	M	T	W	T	F	S
1	2	3	4	5	6	7
8	9	10	11	12	13	14
15	16	17	18	19	20	21
22	23	24	25	26	27	28
29	30	31				

AUGUST 2018

S	M	T	W	T	F	S
			1	2	3	4
5	6	7	8	9	10	11
12	13	14	15	16	17	18
19	20	21	22	23	24	25
26	27	28	29	30	31	

SEPTEMBER 2018

S	M	T	W	T	F	S
						1
2	3	4	5	6	7	8
9	10	11	12	13	14	15
16	17	18	19	20	21	22
23	24	25	26	27	28	29
30						

OCTOBER 2018

S	M	T	W	T	F	S
	1	2	3	4	5	6
7	8	9	10	11	12	13
14	15	16	17	18	19	20
21	22	23	24	25	26	27
28	29	30	31			

NOVEMBER 2018

S	M	T	W	T	F	S
				1	2	3
4	5	6	7	8	9	10
11	12	13	14	15	16	17
18	19	20	21	22	23	24
25	26	27	28	29	30	

DECEMBER 2018

S	M	T	W	T	F	S
						1
2	3	4	5	6	7	8
9	10	11	12	13	14	15
16	17	18	19	20	21	22
23	24	25	26	27	28	29
30	31					

Important Dates

New Year's Eve	December 31
New Year's Day	January 1
Martin Luther King Day	January 15
Groundhog Day	February 2
Presidents' Day	February 12
Valentine's Day	February 14
Ash Wednesday	February 14
Daylight Saving Time begins	March 11
St. Patrick's Day	March 17
Spring Equinox	March 20
Palm Sunday	March 25
Good Friday / First Day of Passover	March 30
Easter Sunday	April 1
Last Day of Passover	April 7
National Day of Prayer	May 3
Mother's Day	May 13
Pentecost	May 20
Memorial Day	May 28
Flag Day	June 14
Father's Day	June 17
Summer Solstice	June 21
Independence Day	July 4
Labor Day	September 3
Rosh Hashanah begins	September 9
Rosh Hashanah ends	September 11
Yom Kippur begins	September 18
Yom Kippur ends	September 19
Autumnal Equinox	September 23
Columbus Day	October 8
Daylight Saving Time ends	November 4
Election Day	November 6
Veterans' Day	November 11
Thanksgiving Day	November 22
First Sunday of Advent / Hanukkah begins	December 2
Hanukkah ends	December 10
Winter Solstice	December 21
Christmas Eve	December 24
Christmas Day	December 25
New Year's Eve	December 31
New Year's Day	January 1

JANUARY

2018

MY GOALS FOR THE MONTH

_____

_____

_____

_____

_____

_____

_____

_____

_____

_____

_____

_____

_____

_____

_____

MONTH AT A GLANCE

MONDAY	1	_____
TUESDAY	2	_____
WEDNESDAY	3	_____
THURSDAY	4	_____
FRIDAY	5	_____
SATURDAY	6	_____
SUNDAY	7	_____
MONDAY	8	_____
TUESDAY	9	_____
WEDNESDAY	10	_____
THURSDAY	11	_____
FRIDAY	12	_____
SATURDAY	13	_____
SUNDAY	14	_____
MONDAY	15	_____
TUESDAY	16	_____
WEDNESDAY	17	_____
THURSDAY	18	_____
FRIDAY	19	_____
SATURDAY	20	_____
SUNDAY	21	_____
MONDAY	22	_____
TUESDAY	23	_____
WEDNESDAY	24	_____
THURSDAY	25	_____
FRIDAY	26	_____
SATURDAY	27	_____
SUNDAY	28	_____
MONDAY	29	_____
TUESDAY	30	_____
WEDNESDAY	31	_____

JAN

JANUARY

*The Lord himself goes before you and will be with you;
he will never leave you nor forsake you.*

Deuteronomy 31:8 NIV

MONDAY 1 New Years Day	TUESDAY 2	WEDNESDAY 3
07:00 AM	07:00 AM	07:00 AM
07:30 AM	07:30 AM	07:30 AM
08:00 AM	08:00 AM	08:00 AM
08:30 AM	08:30 AM	08:30 AM
09:00 AM	09:00 AM	09:00 AM
09:30 AM	09:30 AM	09:30 AM
10:00 AM	10:00 AM	10:00 AM
10:30 AM	10:30 AM	10:30 AM
11:00 AM	11:00 AM	11:00 AM
11:30 AM	11:30 AM	11:30 AM
12:00 PM	12:00 PM	12:00 PM
12:30 PM	12:30 PM	12:30 PM
01:00 PM	01:00 PM	01:00 PM
01:30 PM	01:30 PM	01:30 PM
02:00 PM	02:00 PM	02:00 PM
02:30 PM	02:30 PM	02:30 PM
03:00 PM	03:00 PM	03:00 PM
03:30 PM	03:30 PM	03:30 PM
04:00 PM	04:00 PM	04:00 PM
04:30 PM	04:30 PM	04:30 PM
05:00 PM	05:00 PM	05:00 PM
05:30 PM	05:30 PM	05:30 PM
06:00 PM	06:00 PM	06:00 PM
06:30 PM	06:30 PM	06:30 PM
07:00 PM	07:00 PM	07:00 PM
07:30 PM	07:30 PM	07:30 PM
08:00 PM	08:00 PM	08:00 PM
08:30 PM	08:30 PM	08:30 PM

DECEMBER 2017	JANUARY 2018	FEBRUARY 2018
S M T W T F S	S M T W T F S	S M T W T F S
1 2	1 2 3 4 5 6	1 2 3
3 4 5 6 7 8 9	7 8 9 10 11 12 13	4 5 6 7 8 9 10
10 11 12 13 14 15 16	14 15 16 17 18 19 20	11 12 13 14 15 16 17
17 18 19 20 21 22 23	21 22 23 24 25 26 27	18 19 20 21 22 23 24
24 25 26 27 28 29 30	28 29 30 31	25 26 27 28
31		

JANUARY

THURSDAY 4

07:00 AM
07:30 AM
08:00 AM
08:30 AM
09:00 AM
09:30 AM
10:00 AM
10:30 AM
11:00 AM
11:30 AM
12:00 PM
12:30 PM
01:00 PM
01:30 PM
02:00 PM
02:30 PM
03:00 PM
03:30 PM
04:00 PM
04:30 PM
05:00 PM
05:30 PM
06:00 PM
06:30 PM
07:00 PM
07:30 PM
08:00 PM
08:30 PM

FRIDAY 5

07:00 AM
07:30 AM
08:00 AM
08:30 AM
09:00 AM
09:30 AM
10:00 AM
10:30 AM
11:00 AM
11:30 AM
12:00 PM
12:30 PM
01:00 PM
01:30 PM
02:00 PM
02:30 PM
03:00 PM
03:30 PM
04:00 PM
04:30 PM
05:00 PM
05:30 PM
06:00 PM
06:30 PM
07:00 PM
07:30 PM
08:00 PM
08:30 PM

SATURDAY 6

SUNDAY 7

JANUARY

Prayer Requests

REFLECTIONS

The Lord loves justice and fairness; he will never abandon his people. They will be kept safe forever.

Psalm 37:28 TLB

NOTES

To Do

JANUARY

> *You, God, see the trouble of the afflicted; you consider their grief and take it in hand. The victims commit themselves to you; you are the helper of the fatherless.*
>
> Psalm 10:14 NIV

MONDAY 8	TUESDAY 9	WEDNESDAY 10
07:00 AM	07:00 AM	07:00 AM
07:30 AM	07:30 AM	07:30 AM
08:00 AM	08:00 AM	08:00 AM
08:30 AM	08:30 AM	08:30 AM
09:00 AM	09:00 AM	09:00 AM
09:30 AM	09:30 AM	09:30 AM
10:00 AM	10:00 AM	10:00 AM
10:30 AM	10:30 AM	10:30 AM
11:00 AM	11:00 AM	11:00 AM
11:30 AM	11:30 AM	11:30 AM
12:00 PM	12:00 PM	12:00 PM
12:30 PM	12:30 PM	12:30 PM
01:00 PM	01:00 PM	01:00 PM
01:30 PM	01:30 PM	01:30 PM
02:00 PM	02:00 PM	02:00 PM
02:30 PM	02:30 PM	02:30 PM
03:00 PM	03:00 PM	03:00 PM
03:30 PM	03:30 PM	03:30 PM
04:00 PM	04:00 PM	04:00 PM
04:30 PM	04:30 PM	04:30 PM
05:00 PM	05:00 PM	05:00 PM
05:30 PM	05:30 PM	05:30 PM
06:00 PM	06:00 PM	06:00 PM
06:30 PM	06:30 PM	06:30 PM
07:00 PM	07:00 PM	07:00 PM
07:30 PM	07:30 PM	07:30 PM
08:00 PM	08:00 PM	08:00 PM
08:30 PM	08:30 PM	08:30 PM

JANUARY

DECEMBER 2017

S	M	T	W	T	F	S
					1	2
3	4	5	6	7	8	9
10	11	12	13	14	15	16
17	18	19	20	21	22	23
24	25	26	27	28	29	30
31						

JANUARY 2018

S	M	T	W	T	F	S
	1	2	3	4	5	6
7	8	9	10	11	12	13
14	15	16	17	18	19	20
21	22	23	24	25	26	27
28	29	30	31			

FEBRUARY 2018

S	M	T	W	T	F	S
				1	2	3
4	5	6	7	8	9	10
11	12	13	14	15	16	17
18	19	20	21	22	23	24
25	26	27	28			

THURSDAY 11

07:00 AM
07:30 AM
08:00 AM
08:30 AM
09:00 AM
09:30 AM
10:00 AM
10:30 AM
11:00 AM
11:30 AM
12:00 PM
12:30 PM
01:00 PM
01:30 PM
02:00 PM
02:30 PM
03:00 PM
03:30 PM
04:00 PM
04:30 PM
05:00 PM
05:30 PM
06:00 PM
06:30 PM
07:00 PM
07:30 PM
08:00 PM
08:30 PM

FRIDAY 12

07:00 AM
07:30 AM
08:00 AM
08:30 AM
09:00 AM
09:30 AM
10:00 AM
10:30 AM
11:00 AM
11:30 AM
12:00 PM
12:30 PM
01:00 PM
01:30 PM
02:00 PM
02:30 PM
03:00 PM
03:30 PM
04:00 PM
04:30 PM
05:00 PM
05:30 PM
06:00 PM
06:30 PM
07:00 PM
07:30 PM
08:00 PM
08:30 PM

SATURDAY 13

SUNDAY 14

JANUARY

DECEMBER 2017

S	M	T	W	T	F	S
					1	2
3	4	5	6	7	8	9
10	11	12	13	14	15	16
17	18	19	20	21	22	23
24	25	26	27	28	29	30
31						

JANUARY 2018

S	M	T	W	T	F	S
	1	2	3	4	5	6
7	8	9	10	11	12	13
14	15	16	17	18	19	20
21	22	23	24	25	26	27
28	29	30	31			

FEBRUARY 2018

S	M	T	W	T	F	S
				1	2	3
4	5	6	7	8	9	10
11	12	13	14	15	16	17
18	19	20	21	22	23	24
25	26	27	28			

Prayer Requests

REFLECTIONS

The Lord hears his people when they call to him for help. He rescues them from all their troubles.

Psalm 34:17 NLT

NOTES

To Do

JANUARY

> *The Lord does not see as man sees;*
> *for man looks at the outward appearance, but the*
> *Lord looks at the heart.*
>
> 1 Samuel 16:7 NKJV

MONDAY **15** Martin Luther King Day	TUESDAY **16**	WEDNESDAY **17**
07:00 AM	07:00 AM	07:00 AM
07:30 AM	07:30 AM	07:30 AM
08:00 AM	08:00 AM	08:00 AM
08:30 AM	08:30 AM	08:30 AM
09:00 AM	09:00 AM	09:00 AM
09:30 AM	09:30 AM	09:30 AM
10:00 AM	10:00 AM	10:00 AM
10:30 AM	10:30 AM	10:30 AM
11:00 AM	11:00 AM	11:00 AM
11:30 AM	11:30 AM	11:30 AM
12:00 PM	12:00 PM	12:00 PM
12:30 PM	12:30 PM	12:30 PM
01:00 PM	01:00 PM	01:00 PM
01:30 PM	01:30 PM	01:30 PM
02:00 PM	02:00 PM	02:00 PM
02:30 PM	02:30 PM	02:30 PM
03:00 PM	03:00 PM	03:00 PM
03:30 PM	03:30 PM	03:30 PM
04:00 PM	04:00 PM	04:00 PM
04:30 PM	04:30 PM	04:30 PM
05:00 PM	05:00 PM	05:00 PM
05:30 PM	05:30 PM	05:30 PM
06:00 PM	06:00 PM	06:00 PM
06:30 PM	06:30 PM	06:30 PM
07:00 PM	07:00 PM	07:00 PM
07:30 PM	07:30 PM	07:30 PM
08:00 PM	08:00 PM	08:00 PM
08:30 PM	08:30 PM	08:30 PM

DECEMBER 2017

S	M	T	W	T	F	S
					1	2
3	4	5	6	7	8	9
10	11	12	13	14	15	16
17	18	19	20	21	22	23
24	25	26	27	28	29	30
31						

JANUARY 2018

S	M	T	W	T	F	S
	1	2	3	4	5	6
7	8	9	10	11	12	13
14	15	16	17	18	19	20
21	22	23	24	25	26	27
28	29	30	31			

FEBRUARY 2018

S	M	T	W	T	F	S
				1	2	3
4	5	6	7	8	9	10
11	12	13	14	15	16	17
18	19	20	21	22	23	24
25	26	27	28			

JANUARY

THURSDAY 18

07:00 AM
07:30 AM
08:00 AM
08:30 AM
09:00 AM
09:30 AM
10:00 AM
10:30 AM
11:00 AM
11:30 AM
12:00 PM
12:30 PM
01:00 PM
01:30 PM
02:00 PM
02:30 PM
03:00 PM
03:30 PM
04:00 PM
04:30 PM
05:00 PM
05:30 PM
06:00 PM
06:30 PM
07:00 PM
07:30 PM
08:00 PM
08:30 PM

FRIDAY 19

07:00 AM
07:30 AM
08:00 AM
08:30 AM
09:00 AM
09:30 AM
10:00 AM
10:30 AM
11:00 AM
11:30 AM
12:00 PM
12:30 PM
01:00 PM
01:30 PM
02:00 PM
02:30 PM
03:00 PM
03:30 PM
04:00 PM
04:30 PM
05:00 PM
05:30 PM
06:00 PM
06:30 PM
07:00 PM
07:30 PM
08:00 PM
08:30 PM

SATURDAY 20

SUNDAY 21

JANUARY

DECEMBER 2017

S	M	T	W	T	F	S
					1	2
3	4	5	6	7	8	9
10	11	12	13	14	15	16
17	18	19	20	21	22	23
24	25	26	27	28	29	30
31						

JANUARY 2018

S	M	T	W	T	F	S
	1	2	3	4	5	6
7	8	9	10	11	12	13
14	15	16	17	18	19	20
21	22	23	24	25	26	27
28	29	30	31			

FEBRUARY 2018

S	M	T	W	T	F	S
				1	2	3
4	5	6	7	8	9	10
11	12	13	14	15	16	17
18	19	20	21	22	23	24
25	26	27	28			

Prayer Requests

REFLECTIONS

*If God is for us,
who can be
against us?*

Romans 8:31 ESV

NOTES

To Do

- [ ]
- [ ]
- [ ]
- [ ]
- [ ]
- [ ]
- [ ]
- [ ]
- [ ]
- [ ]
- [ ]
- [ ]
- [ ]
- [ ]
- [ ]
- [ ]

JANUARY

It was for freedom that Christ set us free; therefore keep standing firm and do not be subject again to a yoke of slavery.

Galatians 5:1 NASB

MONDAY 22	TUESDAY 23	WEDNESDAY 24
07:00 AM	07:00 AM	07:00 AM
07:30 AM	07:30 AM	07:30 AM
08:00 AM	08:00 AM	08:00 AM
08:30 AM	08:30 AM	08:30 AM
09:00 AM	09:00 AM	09:00 AM
09:30 AM	09:30 AM	09:30 AM
10:00 AM	10:00 AM	10:00 AM
10:30 AM	10:30 AM	10:30 AM
11:00 AM	11:00 AM	11:00 AM
11:30 AM	11:30 AM	11:30 AM
12:00 PM	12:00 PM	12:00 PM
12:30 PM	12:30 PM	12:30 PM
01:00 PM	01:00 PM	01:00 PM
01:30 PM	01:30 PM	01:30 PM
02:00 PM	02:00 PM	02:00 PM
02:30 PM	02:30 PM	02:30 PM
03:00 PM	03:00 PM	03:00 PM
03:30 PM	03:30 PM	03:30 PM
04:00 PM	04:00 PM	04:00 PM
04:30 PM	04:30 PM	04:30 PM
05:00 PM	05:00 PM	05:00 PM
05:30 PM	05:30 PM	05:30 PM
06:00 PM	06:00 PM	06:00 PM
06:30 PM	06:30 PM	06:30 PM
07:00 PM	07:00 PM	07:00 PM
07:30 PM	07:30 PM	07:30 PM
08:00 PM	08:00 PM	08:00 PM
08:30 PM	08:30 PM	08:30 PM

DECEMBER 2017

S	M	T	W	T	F	S
					1	2
3	4	5	6	7	8	9
10	11	12	13	14	15	16
17	18	19	20	21	22	23
24	25	26	27	28	29	30
31						

JANUARY 2018

S	M	T	W	T	F	S
	1	2	3	4	5	6
7	8	9	10	11	12	13
14	15	16	17	18	19	20
21	22	23	24	25	26	27
28	29	30	31			

FEBRUARY 2018

S	M	T	W	T	F	S
				1	2	3
4	5	6	7	8	9	10
11	12	13	14	15	16	17
18	19	20	21	22	23	24
25	26	27	28			

JANUARY

THURSDAY 25

07:00 AM
07:30 AM
08:00 AM
08:30 AM
09:00 AM
09:30 AM
10:00 AM
10:30 AM
11:00 AM
11:30 AM
12:00 PM
12:30 PM
01:00 PM
01:30 PM
02:00 PM
02:30 PM
03:00 PM
03:30 PM
04:00 PM
04:30 PM
05:00 PM
05:30 PM
06:00 PM
06:30 PM
07:00 PM
07:30 PM
08:00 PM
08:30 PM

FRIDAY 26

07:00 AM
07:30 AM
08:00 AM
08:30 AM
09:00 AM
09:30 AM
10:00 AM
10:30 AM
11:00 AM
11:30 AM
12:00 PM
12:30 PM
01:00 PM
01:30 PM
02:00 PM
02:30 PM
03:00 PM
03:30 PM
04:00 PM
04:30 PM
05:00 PM
05:30 PM
06:00 PM
06:30 PM
07:00 PM
07:30 PM
08:00 PM
08:30 PM

SATURDAY 27

SUNDAY 28

JANUARY

DECEMBER 2017

S	M	T	W	T	F	S
					1	2
3	4	5	6	7	8	9
10	11	12	13	14	15	16
17	18	19	20	21	22	23
24	25	26	27	28	29	30
31						

JANUARY 2018

S	M	T	W	T	F	S
	1	2	3	4	5	6
7	8	9	10	11	12	13
14	15	16	17	18	19	20
21	22	23	24	25	26	27
28	29	30	31			

FEBRUARY 2018

S	M	T	W	T	F	S
				1	2	3
4	5	6	7	8	9	10
11	12	13	14	15	16	17
18	19	20	21	22	23	24
25	26	27	28			

Prayer Requests

REFLECTIONS

Submit to God. Resist the devil and he will flee from you.

James 4:7 NKJV

NOTES

To Do

FEBRUARY

2018

MY GOALS FOR THE MONTH

MONTH AT A GLANCE

THURSDAY	1	
FRIDAY	2	
SATURDAY	3	
SUNDAY	4	
MONDAY	5	
TUESDAY	6	
WEDNESDAY	7	
THURSDAY	8	
FRIDAY	9	
SATURDAY	10	
SUNDAY	11	
MONDAY	12	
TUESDAY	13	
WEDNESDAY	14	
THURSDAY	15	
FRIDAY	16	
SATURDAY	17	
SUNDAY	18	
MONDAY	19	
TUESDAY	20	
WEDNESDAY	21	
THURSDAY	22	
FRIDAY	23	
SATURDAY	24	
SUNDAY	25	
MONDAY	26	
TUESDAY	27	
WEDNESDAY	28	

FEBRUARY

Everyone should be quick to listen, slow to speak and slow to become angry, because human anger does not produce the righteousness that God desires.

James 1:19-20 NIV

MONDAY 29	TUESDAY 30	WEDNESDAY 31
07:00 AM	07:00 AM	07:00 AM
07:30 AM	07:30 AM	07:30 AM
08:00 AM	08:00 AM	08:00 AM
08:30 AM	08:30 AM	08:30 AM
09:00 AM	09:00 AM	09:00 AM
09:30 AM	09:30 AM	09:30 AM
10:00 AM	10:00 AM	10:00 AM
10:30 AM	10:30 AM	10:30 AM
11:00 AM	11:00 AM	11:00 AM
11:30 AM	11:30 AM	11:30 AM
12:00 PM	12:00 PM	12:00 PM
12:30 PM	12:30 PM	12:30 PM
01:00 PM	01:00 PM	01:00 PM
01:30 PM	01:30 PM	01:30 PM
02:00 PM	02:00 PM	02:00 PM
02:30 PM	02:30 PM	02:30 PM
03:00 PM	03:00 PM	03:00 PM
03:30 PM	03:30 PM	03:30 PM
04:00 PM	04:00 PM	04:00 PM
04:30 PM	04:30 PM	04:30 PM
05:00 PM	05:00 PM	05:00 PM
05:30 PM	05:30 PM	05:30 PM
06:00 PM	06:00 PM	06:00 PM
06:30 PM	06:30 PM	06:30 PM
07:00 PM	07:00 PM	07:00 PM
07:30 PM	07:30 PM	07:30 PM
08:00 PM	08:00 PM	08:00 PM
08:30 PM	08:30 PM	08:30 PM

JANUARY 2018

S	M	T	W	T	F	S
	1	2	3	4	5	6
7	8	9	10	11	12	13
14	15	16	17	18	19	20
21	22	23	24	25	26	27
28	29	30	31			

FEBRUARY 2018

S	M	T	W	T	F	S
				1	2	3
4	5	6	7	8	9	10
11	12	13	14	15	16	17
18	19	20	21	22	23	24
25	26	27	28			

MARCH 2018

S	M	T	W	T	F	S
				1	2	3
4	5	6	7	8	9	10
11	12	13	14	15	16	17
18	19	20	21	22	23	24
25	26	27	28	29	30	31

THURSDAY 1

07:00 AM
07:30 AM
08:00 AM
08:30 AM
09:00 AM
09:30 AM
10:00 AM
10:30 AM
11:00 AM
11:30 AM
12:00 PM
12:30 PM
01:00 PM
01:30 PM
02:00 PM
02:30 PM
03:00 PM
03:30 PM
04:00 PM
04:30 PM
05:00 PM
05:30 PM
06:00 PM
06:30 PM
07:00 PM
07:30 PM
08:00 PM
08:30 PM

FRIDAY 2

Groundhog Day

07:00 AM
07:30 AM
08:00 AM
08:30 AM
09:00 AM
09:30 AM
10:00 AM
10:30 AM
11:00 AM
11:30 AM
12:00 PM
12:30 PM
01:00 PM
01:30 PM
02:00 PM
02:30 PM
03:00 PM
03:30 PM
04:00 PM
04:30 PM
05:00 PM
05:30 PM
06:00 PM
06:30 PM
07:00 PM
07:30 PM
08:00 PM
08:30 PM

SATURDAY 3

SUNDAY 4

FEBRUARY

JANUARY 2018
S	M	T	W	T	F	S
	1	2	3	4	5	6
7	8	9	10	11	12	13
14	15	16	17	18	19	20
21	22	23	24	25	26	27
28	29	30	31			

FEBRUARY 2018
S	M	T	W	T	F	S
				1	2	3
4	5	6	7	8	9	10
11	12	13	14	15	16	17
18	19	20	21	22	23	24
25	26	27	28			

MARCH 2018
S	M	T	W	T	F	S
				1	2	3
4	5	6	7	8	9	10
11	12	13	14	15	16	17
18	19	20	21	22	23	24
25	26	27	28	29	30	31

F
E
B

Prayer Requests

REFLECTIONS

*Those with good
sense are slow
to anger, and
it is their glory
to overlook an
offense.*

Proverbs 19:11 NRSV

NOTES

To Do

- [ ]
- [ ]
- [ ]
- [ ]
- [ ]
- [ ]
- [ ]
- [ ]
- [ ]
- [ ]
- [ ]
- [ ]
- [ ]
- [ ]
- [ ]

FEBRUARY

> *Cast all your anxiety on him,*
> *because he cares for you.*
>
> 1 Peter 5:7 NRSV

MONDAY 5	TUESDAY 6	WEDNESDAY 7
07:00 AM	07:00 AM	07:00 AM
07:30 AM	07:30 AM	07:30 AM
08:00 AM	08:00 AM	08:00 AM
08:30 AM	08:30 AM	08:30 AM
09:00 AM	09:00 AM	09:00 AM
09:30 AM	09:30 AM	09:30 AM
10:00 AM	10:00 AM	10:00 AM
10:30 AM	10:30 AM	10:30 AM
11:00 AM	11:00 AM	11:00 AM
11:30 AM	11:30 AM	11:30 AM
12:00 PM	12:00 PM	12:00 PM
12:30 PM	12:30 PM	12:30 PM
01:00 PM	01:00 PM	01:00 PM
01:30 PM	01:30 PM	01:30 PM
02:00 PM	02:00 PM	02:00 PM
02:30 PM	02:30 PM	02:30 PM
03:00 PM	03:00 PM	03:00 PM
03:30 PM	03:30 PM	03:30 PM
04:00 PM	04:00 PM	04:00 PM
04:30 PM	04:30 PM	04:30 PM
05:00 PM	05:00 PM	05:00 PM
05:30 PM	05:30 PM	05:30 PM
06:00 PM	06:00 PM	06:00 PM
06:30 PM	06:30 PM	06:30 PM
07:00 PM	07:00 PM	07:00 PM
07:30 PM	07:30 PM	07:30 PM
08:00 PM	08:00 PM	08:00 PM
08:30 PM	08:30 PM	08:30 PM

JANUARY 2018
S M T W T F S
1 2 3 4 5 6
7 8 9 10 11 12 13
14 15 16 17 18 19 20
21 22 23 24 25 26 27
28 29 30 31

FEBRUARY 2018
S M T W T F S
1 2 3
4 5 6 7 8 9 10
11 12 13 14 15 16 17
18 19 20 21 22 23 24
25 26 27 28

MARCH 2018
S M T W T F S
1 2 3
4 5 6 7 8 9 10
11 12 13 14 15 16 17
18 19 20 21 22 23 24
25 26 27 28 29 30 31

FEBRUARY

F E B

THURSDAY 8

07:00 AM	
07:30 AM	
08:00 AM	
08:30 AM	
09:00 AM	
09:30 AM	
10:00 AM	
10:30 AM	
11:00 AM	
11:30 AM	
12:00 PM	
12:30 PM	
01:00 PM	
01:30 PM	
02:00 PM	
02:30 PM	
03:00 PM	
03:30 PM	
04:00 PM	
04:30 PM	
05:00 PM	
05:30 PM	
06:00 PM	
06:30 PM	
07:00 PM	
07:30 PM	
08:00 PM	
08:30 PM	

FRIDAY 9

07:00 AM	
07:30 AM	
08:00 AM	
08:30 AM	
09:00 AM	
09:30 AM	
10:00 AM	
10:30 AM	
11:00 AM	
11:30 AM	
12:00 PM	
12:30 PM	
01:00 PM	
01:30 PM	
02:00 PM	
02:30 PM	
03:00 PM	
03:30 PM	
04:00 PM	
04:30 PM	
05:00 PM	
05:30 PM	
06:00 PM	
06:30 PM	
07:00 PM	
07:30 PM	
08:00 PM	
08:30 PM	

SATURDAY 10

SUNDAY 11

FEBRUARY

JANUARY 2018

S	M	T	W	T	F	S
	1	2	3	4	5	6
7	8	9	10	11	12	13
14	15	16	17	18	19	20
21	22	23	24	25	26	27
28	29	30	31			

FEBRUARY 2018

S	M	T	W	T	F	S
				1	2	3
4	5	6	7	8	9	10
11	12	13	14	15	16	17
18	19	20	21	22	23	24
25	26	27	28			

MARCH 2018

S	M	T	W	T	F	S
				1	2	3
4	5	6	7	8	9	10
11	12	13	14	15	16	17
18	19	20	21	22	23	24
25	26	27	28	29	30	31

Prayer Requests

REFLECTIONS

You keep him in perfect peace whose mind is stayed on you, because he trusts in you.

Isaiah 26:3 ESV

NOTES

To Do

FEBRUARY

> *To all who did accept him and believe in him he gave the right to become children of God.*
>
> John 1:12 NCV

MONDAY
12 — Presidents' Day

07:00 AM
07:30 AM
08:00 AM
08:30 AM
09:00 AM
09:30 AM
10:00 AM
10:30 AM
11:00 AM
11:30 AM
12:00 PM
12:30 PM
01:00 PM
01:30 PM
02:00 PM
02:30 PM
03:00 PM
03:30 PM
04:00 PM
04:30 PM
05:00 PM
05:30 PM
06:00 PM
06:30 PM
07:00 PM
07:30 PM
08:00 PM
08:30 PM

TUESDAY
13

07:00 AM
07:30 AM
08:00 AM
08:30 AM
09:00 AM
09:30 AM
10:00 AM
10:30 AM
11:00 AM
11:30 AM
12:00 PM
12:30 PM
01:00 PM
01:30 PM
02:00 PM
02:30 PM
03:00 PM
03:30 PM
04:00 PM
04:30 PM
05:00 PM
05:30 PM
06:00 PM
06:30 PM
07:00 PM
07:30 PM
08:00 PM
08:30 PM

WEDNESDAY
14 — Valentine's Day / Ash Wednesday

07:00 AM
07:30 AM
08:00 AM
08:30 AM
09:00 AM
09:30 AM
10:00 AM
10:30 AM
11:00 AM
11:30 AM
12:00 PM
12:30 PM
01:00 PM
01:30 PM
02:00 PM
02:30 PM
03:00 PM
03:30 PM
04:00 PM
04:30 PM
05:00 PM
05:30 PM
06:00 PM
06:30 PM
07:00 PM
07:30 PM
08:00 PM
08:30 PM

JANUARY 2018	FEBRUARY 2018	MARCH 2018
S M T W T F S	S M T W T F S	S M T W T F S
1 2 3 4 5 6	1 2 3	1 2 3
7 8 9 10 11 12 13	4 5 6 7 8 9 10	4 5 6 7 8 9 10
14 15 16 17 18 19 20	11 12 13 14 15 16 17	11 12 13 14 15 16 17
21 22 23 24 25 26 27	18 19 20 21 22 23 24	18 19 20 21 22 23 24
28 29 30 31	25 26 27 28	25 26 27 28 29 30 31

FEBRUARY

FEB

THURSDAY 15

07:00 AM	
07:30 AM	
08:00 AM	
08:30 AM	
09:00 AM	
09:30 AM	
10:00 AM	
10:30 AM	
11:00 AM	
11:30 AM	
12:00 PM	
12:30 PM	
01:00 PM	
01:30 PM	
02:00 PM	
02:30 PM	
03:00 PM	
03:30 PM	
04:00 PM	
04:30 PM	
05:00 PM	
05:30 PM	
06:00 PM	
06:30 PM	
07:00 PM	
07:30 PM	
08:00 PM	
08:30 PM	

FRIDAY 16

07:00 AM	
07:30 AM	
08:00 AM	
08:30 AM	
09:00 AM	
09:30 AM	
10:00 AM	
10:30 AM	
11:00 AM	
11:30 AM	
12:00 PM	
12:30 PM	
01:00 PM	
01:30 PM	
02:00 PM	
02:30 PM	
03:00 PM	
03:30 PM	
04:00 PM	
04:30 PM	
05:00 PM	
05:30 PM	
06:00 PM	
06:30 PM	
07:00 PM	
07:30 PM	
08:00 PM	
08:30 PM	

SATURDAY 17

SUNDAY 18

FEBRUARY

F
E
B

JANUARY 2018

S	M	T	W	T	F	S
	1	2	3	4	5	6
7	8	9	10	11	12	13
14	15	16	17	18	19	20
21	22	23	24	25	26	27
28	29	30	31			

FEBRUARY 2018

S	M	T	W	T	F	S
				1	2	3
4	5	6	7	8	9	10
11	12	13	14	15	16	17
18	19	20	21	22	23	24
25	26	27	28			

MARCH 2018

S	M	T	W	T	F	S
				1	2	3
4	5	6	7	8	9	10
11	12	13	14	15	16	17
18	19	20	21	22	23	24
25	26	27	28	29	30	31

Prayer Requests

REFLECTIONS

"Blessed are those who have not seen and yet have believed."

John 20:29 ESV

NOTES

To Do

FEBRUARY

> *You, O LORD, will bless the righteous;*
> *With favor You will surround him as with a shield.*
>
> Psalm 5:12 NKJV

MONDAY 19 — Presidents' Day

07:00 AM
07:30 AM
08:00 AM
08:30 AM
09:00 AM
09:30 AM
10:00 AM
10:30 AM
11:00 AM
11:30 AM
12:00 PM
12:30 PM
01:00 PM
01:30 PM
02:00 PM
02:30 PM
03:00 PM
03:30 PM
04:00 PM
04:30 PM
05:00 PM
05:30 PM
06:00 PM
06:30 PM
07:00 PM
07:30 PM
08:00 PM
08:30 PM

TUESDAY 20

07:00 AM
07:30 AM
08:00 AM
08:30 AM
09:00 AM
09:30 AM
10:00 AM
10:30 AM
11:00 AM
11:30 AM
12:00 PM
12:30 PM
01:00 PM
01:30 PM
02:00 PM
02:30 PM
03:00 PM
03:30 PM
04:00 PM
04:30 PM
05:00 PM
05:30 PM
06:00 PM
06:30 PM
07:00 PM
07:30 PM
08:00 PM
08:30 PM

WEDNESDAY 21

07:00 AM
07:30 AM
08:00 AM
08:30 AM
09:00 AM
09:30 AM
10:00 AM
10:30 AM
11:00 AM
11:30 AM
12:00 PM
12:30 PM
01:00 PM
01:30 PM
02:00 PM
02:30 PM
03:00 PM
03:30 PM
04:00 PM
04:30 PM
05:00 PM
05:30 PM
06:00 PM
06:30 PM
07:00 PM
07:30 PM
08:00 PM
08:30 PM

JANUARY 2018						
S	M	T	W	T	F	S
	1	2	3	4	5	6
7	8	9	10	11	12	13
14	15	16	17	18	19	20
21	22	23	24	25	26	27
28	29	30	31			

FEBRUARY 2018						
S	M	T	W	T	F	S
				1	2	3
4	5	6	7	8	9	10
11	12	13	14	15	16	17
18	19	20	21	22	23	24
25	26	27	28			

MARCH 2018						
S	M	T	W	T	F	S
				1	2	3
4	5	6	7	8	9	10
11	12	13	14	15	16	17
18	19	20	21	22	23	24
25	26	27	28	29	30	31

FEBRUARY

FEB

THURSDAY 22

07:00 AM
07:30 AM
08:00 AM
08:30 AM
09:00 AM
09:30 AM
10:00 AM
10:30 AM
11:00 AM
11:30 AM
12:00 PM
12:30 PM
01:00 PM
01:30 PM
02:00 PM
02:30 PM
03:00 PM
03:30 PM
04:00 PM
04:30 PM
05:00 PM
05:30 PM
06:00 PM
06:30 PM
07:00 PM
07:30 PM
08:00 PM
08:30 PM

FRIDAY 23

07:00 AM
07:30 AM
08:00 AM
08:30 AM
09:00 AM
09:30 AM
10:00 AM
10:30 AM
11:00 AM
11:30 AM
12:00 PM
12:30 PM
01:00 PM
01:30 PM
02:00 PM
02:30 PM
03:00 PM
03:30 PM
04:00 PM
04:30 PM
05:00 PM
05:30 PM
06:00 PM
06:30 PM
07:00 PM
07:30 PM
08:00 PM
08:30 PM

SATURDAY 24

SUNDAY 25

FEBRUARY

JANUARY 2018						
S	M	T	W	T	F	S
	1	2	3	4	5	6
7	8	9	10	11	12	13
14	15	16	17	18	19	20
21	22	23	24	25	26	27
28	29	30	31			

FEBRUARY 2018						
S	M	T	W	T	F	S
				1	2	3
4	5	6	7	8	9	10
11	12	13	14	15	16	17
18	19	20	21	22	23	24
25	26	27	28			

MARCH 2018						
S	M	T	W	T	F	S
				1	2	3
4	5	6	7	8	9	10
11	12	13	14	15	16	17
18	19	20	21	22	23	24
25	26	27	28	29	30	31

Prayer Requests

REFLECTIONS

Surely you have granted him unending blessings and made him glad with the joy of your presence.

Psalm 21:6 NIV

NOTES

To Do

- [ ]
- [ ]
- [ ]
- [ ]
- [ ]
- [ ]
- [ ]
- [ ]
- [ ]
- [ ]
- [ ]
- [ ]
- [ ]
- [ ]

MARCH

2018

Blessed be the God and Father of our Lord Jesus Christ, who has blessed us in Christ with every spiritual blessing in the heavenly places, even as he chose us in him before the foundation of the world, that we should be holy and blameless before him.

EPHESIANS 1:3-4 ESV

MY GOALS FOR THE MONTH

MONTH AT A GLANCE

THURSDAY	1	
FRIDAY	2	
SATURDAY	3	
SUNDAY	4	
MONDAY	5	
TUESDAY	6	
WEDNESDAY	7	
THURSDAY	8	
FRIDAY	9	
SATURDAY	10	
SUNDAY	11	
MONDAY	12	
TUESDAY	13	
WEDNESDAY	14	
THURSDAY	15	
FRIDAY	16	
SATURDAY	17	
SUNDAY	18	
MONDAY	19	
TUESDAY	20	
WEDNESDAY	21	
THURSDAY	22	
FRIDAY	23	
SATURDAY	24	
SUNDAY	25	
MONDAY	26	
TUESDAY	27	
WEDNESDAY	28	
THURSDAY	29	
FRIDAY	30	
SATURDAY	31	

FEBRUARY

> *Do not merely look out for your own personal interests, but also for the interests of others.*
>
> Philippians 2:4 NASB

MONDAY
26

07:00 AM	
07:30 AM	
08:00 AM	
08:30 AM	
09:00 AM	
09:30 AM	
10:00 AM	
10:30 AM	
11:00 AM	
11:30 AM	
12:00 PM	
12:30 PM	
01:00 PM	
01:30 PM	
02:00 PM	
02:30 PM	
03:00 PM	
03:30 PM	
04:00 PM	
04:30 PM	
05:00 PM	
05:30 PM	
06:00 PM	
06:30 PM	
07:00 PM	
07:30 PM	
08:00 PM	
08:30 PM	

TUESDAY
27

07:00 AM	
07:30 AM	
08:00 AM	
08:30 AM	
09:00 AM	
09:30 AM	
10:00 AM	
10:30 AM	
11:00 AM	
11:30 AM	
12:00 PM	
12:30 PM	
01:00 PM	
01:30 PM	
02:00 PM	
02:30 PM	
03:00 PM	
03:30 PM	
04:00 PM	
04:30 PM	
05:00 PM	
05:30 PM	
06:00 PM	
06:30 PM	
07:00 PM	
07:30 PM	
08:00 PM	
08:30 PM	

WEDNESDAY
28 Ash Wednesday

07:00 AM	
07:30 AM	
08:00 AM	
08:30 AM	
09:00 AM	
09:30 AM	
10:00 AM	
10:30 AM	
11:00 AM	
11:30 AM	
12:00 PM	
12:30 PM	
01:00 PM	
01:30 PM	
02:00 PM	
02:30 PM	
03:00 PM	
03:30 PM	
04:00 PM	
04:30 PM	
05:00 PM	
05:30 PM	
06:00 PM	
06:30 PM	
07:00 PM	
07:30 PM	
08:00 PM	
08:30 PM	

FEBRUARY 2018

S	M	T	W	T	F	S
				1	2	3
4	5	6	7	8	9	10
11	12	13	14	15	16	17
18	19	20	21	22	23	24
25	26	27	28			

MARCH 2018

S	M	T	W	T	F	S
				1	2	3
4	5	6	7	8	9	10
11	12	13	14	15	16	17
18	19	20	21	22	23	24
25	26	27	28	29	30	31

APRIL 2018

S	M	T	W	T	F	S
1	2	3	4	5	6	7
8	9	10	11	12	13	14
15	16	17	18	19	20	21
22	23	24	25	26	27	28
29	30					

THURSDAY 1

- 07:00 AM
- 07:30 AM
- 08:00 AM
- 08:30 AM
- 09:00 AM
- 09:30 AM
- 10:00 AM
- 10:30 AM
- 11:00 AM
- 11:30 AM
- 12:00 PM
- 12:30 PM
- 01:00 PM
- 01:30 PM
- 02:00 PM
- 02:30 PM
- 03:00 PM
- 03:30 PM
- 04:00 PM
- 04:30 PM
- 05:00 PM
- 05:30 PM
- 06:00 PM
- 06:30 PM
- 07:00 PM
- 07:30 PM
- 08:00 PM
- 08:30 PM

FRIDAY 2

- 07:00 AM
- 07:30 AM
- 08:00 AM
- 08:30 AM
- 09:00 AM
- 09:30 AM
- 10:00 AM
- 10:30 AM
- 11:00 AM
- 11:30 AM
- 12:00 PM
- 12:30 PM
- 01:00 PM
- 01:30 PM
- 02:00 PM
- 02:30 PM
- 03:00 PM
- 03:30 PM
- 04:00 PM
- 04:30 PM
- 05:00 PM
- 05:30 PM
- 06:00 PM
- 06:30 PM
- 07:00 PM
- 07:30 PM
- 08:00 PM
- 08:30 PM

SATURDAY 3

SUNDAY 4

MARCH

FEBRUARY 2018

S	M	T	W	T	F	S
				1	2	3
4	5	6	7	8	9	10
11	12	13	14	15	16	17
18	19	20	21	22	23	24
25	26	27	28			

MARCH 2018

S	M	T	W	T	F	S
				1	2	3
4	5	6	7	8	9	10
11	12	13	14	15	16	17
18	19	20	21	22	23	24
25	26	27	28	29	30	31

APRIL 2018

S	M	T	W	T	F	S
1	2	3	4	5	6	7
8	9	10	11	12	13	14
15	16	17	18	19	20	21
22	23	24	25	26	27	28
29	30					

Prayer Requests

REFLECTIONS

Religion that is pure and undefiled before God, the Father, is this: to care for orphans and widows in their distress, and to keep oneself unstained by the world.

James 1:27 NRSV

NOTES

To Do

MARCH

> *Jesus Christ is the same yesterday and today and forever.*
>
> Hebrews 13:8 NASB

MONDAY 5	TUESDAY 6	WEDNESDAY 7
07:00 AM	07:00 AM	07:00 AM
07:30 AM	07:30 AM	07:30 AM
08:00 AM	08:00 AM	08:00 AM
08:30 AM	08:30 AM	08:30 AM
09:00 AM	09:00 AM	09:00 AM
09:30 AM	09:30 AM	09:30 AM
10:00 AM	10:00 AM	10:00 AM
10:30 AM	10:30 AM	10:30 AM
11:00 AM	11:00 AM	11:00 AM
11:30 AM	11:30 AM	11:30 AM
12:00 PM	12:00 PM	12:00 PM
12:30 PM	12:30 PM	12:30 PM
01:00 PM	01:00 PM	01:00 PM
01:30 PM	01:30 PM	01:30 PM
02:00 PM	02:00 PM	02:00 PM
02:30 PM	02:30 PM	02:30 PM
03:00 PM	03:00 PM	03:00 PM
03:30 PM	03:30 PM	03:30 PM
04:00 PM	04:00 PM	04:00 PM
04:30 PM	04:30 PM	04:30 PM
05:00 PM	05:00 PM	05:00 PM
05:30 PM	05:30 PM	05:30 PM
06:00 PM	06:00 PM	06:00 PM
06:30 PM	06:30 PM	06:30 PM
07:00 PM	07:00 PM	07:00 PM
07:30 PM	07:30 PM	07:30 PM
08:00 PM	08:00 PM	08:00 PM
08:30 PM	08:30 PM	08:30 PM

FEBRUARY 2018

S	M	T	W	T	F	S
				1	2	3
4	5	6	7	8	9	10
11	12	13	14	15	16	17
18	19	20	21	22	23	24
25	26	27	28			

MARCH 2018

S	M	T	W	T	F	S
				1	2	3
4	5	6	7	8	9	10
11	12	13	14	15	16	17
18	19	20	21	22	23	24
25	26	27	28	29	30	31

APRIL 2018

S	M	T	W	T	F	S
1	2	3	4	5	6	7
8	9	10	11	12	13	14
15	16	17	18	19	20	21
22	23	24	25	26	27	28
29	30					

THURSDAY 8

07:00 AM
07:30 AM
08:00 AM
08:30 AM
09:00 AM
09:30 AM
10:00 AM
10:30 AM
11:00 AM
11:30 AM
12:00 PM
12:30 PM
01:00 PM
01:30 PM
02:00 PM
02:30 PM
03:00 PM
03:30 PM
04:00 PM
04:30 PM
05:00 PM
05:30 PM
06:00 PM
06:30 PM
07:00 PM
07:30 PM
08:00 PM
08:30 PM

FRIDAY 9

07:00 AM
07:30 AM
08:00 AM
08:30 AM
09:00 AM
09:30 AM
10:00 AM
10:30 AM
11:00 AM
11:30 AM
12:00 PM
12:30 PM
01:00 PM
01:30 PM
02:00 PM
02:30 PM
03:00 PM
03:30 PM
04:00 PM
04:30 PM
05:00 PM
05:30 PM
06:00 PM
06:30 PM
07:00 PM
07:30 PM
08:00 PM
08:30 PM

SATURDAY 10

SUNDAY 11

Daylight Saving
Time begins

MARCH

FEBRUARY 2018						
S	M	T	W	T	F	S
					1	2	3
4	5	6	7	8	9	10
11	12	13	14	15	16	17
18	19	20	21	22	23	24
25	26	27	28			

MARCH 2018						
S	M	T	W	T	F	S
					1	2	3
4	5	6	7	8	9	10
11	12	13	14	15	16	17
18	19	20	21	22	23	24
25	26	27	28	29	30	31

APRIL 2018						
S	M	T	W	T	F	S
1	2	3	4	5	6	7
8	9	10	11	12	13	14
15	16	17	18	19	20	21
22	23	24	25	26	27	28
29	30					

Prayer Requests

REFLECTIONS

Every good gift and every perfect gift is from above, coming down from the Father of lights with whom there is no variation or shadow due to change.

James 1:17 ESV

NOTES

To Do

MARCH

> *Commit your work to the Lord,*
> *and your plans will be established.*
>
> Proverbs 16:3 ESV

MAR

MONDAY 12	TUESDAY 13	WEDNESDAY 14
07:00 AM	07:00 AM	07:00 AM
07:30 AM	07:30 AM	07:30 AM
08:00 AM	08:00 AM	08:00 AM
08:30 AM	08:30 AM	08:30 AM
09:00 AM	09:00 AM	09:00 AM
09:30 AM	09:30 AM	09:30 AM
10:00 AM	10:00 AM	10:00 AM
10:30 AM	10:30 AM	10:30 AM
11:00 AM	11:00 AM	11:00 AM
11:30 AM	11:30 AM	11:30 AM
12:00 PM	12:00 PM	12:00 PM
12:30 PM	12:30 PM	12:30 PM
01:00 PM	01:00 PM	01:00 PM
01:30 PM	01:30 PM	01:30 PM
02:00 PM	02:00 PM	02:00 PM
02:30 PM	02:30 PM	02:30 PM
03:00 PM	03:00 PM	03:00 PM
03:30 PM	03:30 PM	03:30 PM
04:00 PM	04:00 PM	04:00 PM
04:30 PM	04:30 PM	04:30 PM
05:00 PM	05:00 PM	05:00 PM
05:30 PM	05:30 PM	05:30 PM
06:00 PM	06:00 PM	06:00 PM
06:30 PM	06:30 PM	06:30 PM
07:00 PM	07:00 PM	07:00 PM
07:30 PM	07:30 PM	07:30 PM
08:00 PM	08:00 PM	08:00 PM
08:30 PM	08:30 PM	08:30 PM

FEBRUARY 2018	MARCH 2018	APRIL 2018
S M T W T F S	S M T W T F S	S M T W T F S
1 2 3	1 2 3	1 2 3 4 5 6 7
4 5 6 7 8 9 10	4 5 6 7 8 9 10	8 9 10 11 12 13 14
11 12 13 14 15 16 17	11 12 13 14 15 16 17	15 16 17 18 19 20 21
18 19 20 21 22 23 24	18 19 20 21 22 23 24	22 23 24 25 26 27 28
25 26 27 28	25 26 27 28 29 30 31	29 30

MARCH

MAR

THURSDAY 15

07:00 AM	
07:30 AM	
08:00 AM	
08:30 AM	
09:00 AM	
09:30 AM	
10:00 AM	
10:30 AM	
11:00 AM	
11:30 AM	
12:00 PM	
12:30 PM	
01:00 PM	
01:30 PM	
02:00 PM	
02:30 PM	
03:00 PM	
03:30 PM	
04:00 PM	
04:30 PM	
05:00 PM	
05:30 PM	
06:00 PM	
06:30 PM	
07:00 PM	
07:30 PM	
08:00 PM	
08:30 PM	

FRIDAY 16

07:00 AM	
07:30 AM	
08:00 AM	
08:30 AM	
09:00 AM	
09:30 AM	
10:00 AM	
10:30 AM	
11:00 AM	
11:30 AM	
12:00 PM	
12:30 PM	
01:00 PM	
01:30 PM	
02:00 PM	
02:30 PM	
03:00 PM	
03:30 PM	
04:00 PM	
04:30 PM	
05:00 PM	
05:30 PM	
06:00 PM	
06:30 PM	
07:00 PM	
07:30 PM	
08:00 PM	
08:30 PM	

SATURDAY 17

St. Patrick's Day

SUNDAY 18

MARCH

FEBRUARY 2018						
S	M	T	W	T	F	S
				1	2	3
4	5	6	7	8	9	10
11	12	13	14	15	16	17
18	19	20	21	22	23	24
25	26	27	28			

MARCH 2018						
S	M	T	W	T	F	S
				1	2	3
4	5	6	7	8	9	10
11	12	13	14	15	16	17
18	19	20	21	22	23	24
25	26	27	28	29	30	31

APRIL 2018						
S	M	T	W	T	F	S
1	2	3	4	5	6	7
8	9	10	11	12	13	14
15	16	17	18	19	20	21
22	23	24	25	26	27	28
29	30					

Prayer Requests

REFLECTIONS

"Seek first the kingdom of God and His righteousness, and all these things shall be added to you."

Matthew 6:33 NKJV

NOTES

To Do

MARCH

> *Praise be to the God and Father of our Lord Jesus Christ, the Father of compassion and the God of all comfort.*
>
> 2 Corinthians 1:3 NIV

MONDAY **19**	TUESDAY **20** Spring Equinox	WEDNESDAY **21**
07:00 AM	07:00 AM	07:00 AM
07:30 AM	07:30 AM	07:30 AM
08:00 AM	08:00 AM	08:00 AM
08:30 AM	08:30 AM	08:30 AM
09:00 AM	09:00 AM	09:00 AM
09:30 AM	09:30 AM	09:30 AM
10:00 AM	10:00 AM	10:00 AM
10:30 AM	10:30 AM	10:30 AM
11:00 AM	11:00 AM	11:00 AM
11:30 AM	11:30 AM	11:30 AM
12:00 PM	12:00 PM	12:00 PM
12:30 PM	12:30 PM	12:30 PM
01:00 PM	01:00 PM	01:00 PM
01:30 PM	01:30 PM	01:30 PM
02:00 PM	02:00 PM	02:00 PM
02:30 PM	02:30 PM	02:30 PM
03:00 PM	03:00 PM	03:00 PM
03:30 PM	03:30 PM	03:30 PM
04:00 PM	04:00 PM	04:00 PM
04:30 PM	04:30 PM	04:30 PM
05:00 PM	05:00 PM	05:00 PM
05:30 PM	05:30 PM	05:30 PM
06:00 PM	06:00 PM	06:00 PM
06:30 PM	06:30 PM	06:30 PM
07:00 PM	07:00 PM	07:00 PM
07:30 PM	07:30 PM	07:30 PM
08:00 PM	08:00 PM	08:00 PM
08:30 PM	08:30 PM	08:30 PM

FEBRUARY 2018						
S	M	T	W	T	F	S
				1	2	3
4	5	6	7	8	9	10
11	12	13	14	15	16	17
18	19	20	21	22	23	24
25	26	27	28			

MARCH 2018						
S	M	T	W	T	F	S
				1	2	3
4	5	6	7	8	9	10
11	12	13	14	15	16	17
18	19	20	21	22	23	24
25	26	27	28	29	30	31

APRIL 2018						
S	M	T	W	T	F	S
1	2	3	4	5	6	7
8	9	10	11	12	13	14
15	16	17	18	19	20	21
22	23	24	25	26	27	28
29	30					

MARCH

MAR

THURSDAY 22

- 07:00 AM
- 07:30 AM
- 08:00 AM
- 08:30 AM
- 09:00 AM
- 09:30 AM
- 10:00 AM
- 10:30 AM
- 11:00 AM
- 11:30 AM
- 12:00 PM
- 12:30 PM
- 01:00 PM
- 01:30 PM
- 02:00 PM
- 02:30 PM
- 03:00 PM
- 03:30 PM
- 04:00 PM
- 04:30 PM
- 05:00 PM
- 05:30 PM
- 06:00 PM
- 06:30 PM
- 07:00 PM
- 07:30 PM
- 08:00 PM
- 08:30 PM

FRIDAY 23

- 07:00 AM
- 07:30 AM
- 08:00 AM
- 08:30 AM
- 09:00 AM
- 09:30 AM
- 10:00 AM
- 10:30 AM
- 11:00 AM
- 11:30 AM
- 12:00 PM
- 12:30 PM
- 01:00 PM
- 01:30 PM
- 02:00 PM
- 02:30 PM
- 03:00 PM
- 03:30 PM
- 04:00 PM
- 04:30 PM
- 05:00 PM
- 05:30 PM
- 06:00 PM
- 06:30 PM
- 07:00 PM
- 07:30 PM
- 08:00 PM
- 08:30 PM

SATURDAY 24

SUNDAY 25   Palm Sunday

MARCH

FEBRUARY 2018

S	M	T	W	T	F	S
				1	2	3
4	5	6	7	8	9	10
11	12	13	14	15	16	17
18	19	20	21	22	23	24
25	26	27	28			

MARCH 2018

S	M	T	W	T	F	S
				1	2	3
4	5	6	7	8	9	10
11	12	13	14	15	16	17
18	19	20	21	22	23	24
25	26	27	28	29	30	31

APRIL 2018

S	M	T	W	T	F	S
1	2	3	4	5	6	7
8	9	10	11	12	13	14
15	16	17	18	19	20	21
22	23	24	25	26	27	28
29	30					

MAR

Prayer Requests

_____
_____
_____
_____
_____
_____
_____
_____
_____
_____

REFLECTIONS

The Lord longs to be gracious to you; Therefore he will rise up to show you compassion. For the Lord is a God of justice. Blessed are all who wait for him!

Isaiah 30:18 NIV

NOTES

To Do

☐

☐

☐

☐

☐

☐

☐

☐

☐

☐

☐

☐

☐

☐

☐

MARCH

I am confident of this very thing, that He who began a good work in you will perfect it until the day of Christ Jesus.

Philippians 1:6 NASB

MAR

MONDAY 26

07:00 AM
07:30 AM
08:00 AM
08:30 AM
09:00 AM
09:30 AM
10:00 AM
10:30 AM
11:00 AM
11:30 AM
12:00 PM
12:30 PM
01:00 PM
01:30 PM
02:00 PM
02:30 PM
03:00 PM
03:30 PM
04:00 PM
04:30 PM
05:00 PM
05:30 PM
06:00 PM
06:30 PM
07:00 PM
07:30 PM
08:00 PM
08:30 PM

TUESDAY 27

07:00 AM
07:30 AM
08:00 AM
08:30 AM
09:00 AM
09:30 AM
10:00 AM
10:30 AM
11:00 AM
11:30 AM
12:00 PM
12:30 PM
01:00 PM
01:30 PM
02:00 PM
02:30 PM
03:00 PM
03:30 PM
04:00 PM
04:30 PM
05:00 PM
05:30 PM
06:00 PM
06:30 PM
07:00 PM
07:30 PM
08:00 PM
08:30 PM

WEDNESDAY 28

07:00 AM
07:30 AM
08:00 AM
08:30 AM
09:00 AM
09:30 AM
10:00 AM
10:30 AM
11:00 AM
11:30 AM
12:00 PM
12:30 PM
01:00 PM
01:30 PM
02:00 PM
02:30 PM
03:00 PM
03:30 PM
04:00 PM
04:30 PM
05:00 PM
05:30 PM
06:00 PM
06:30 PM
07:00 PM
07:30 PM
08:00 PM
08:30 PM

FEBRUARY 2018

S	M	T	W	T	F	S
				1	2	3
4	5	6	7	8	9	10
11	12	13	14	15	16	17
18	19	20	21	22	23	24
25	26	27	28			

MARCH 2018

S	M	T	W	T	F	S
				1	2	3
4	5	6	7	8	9	10
11	12	13	14	15	16	17
18	19	20	21	22	23	24
25	26	27	28	29	30	31

APRIL 2018

S	M	T	W	T	F	S
1	2	3	4	5	6	7
8	9	10	11	12	13	14
15	16	17	18	19	20	21
22	23	24	25	26	27	28
29	30					

THURSDAY 29

07:00 AM
07:30 AM
08:00 AM
08:30 AM
09:00 AM
09:30 AM
10:00 AM
10:30 AM
11:00 AM
11:30 AM
12:00 PM
12:30 PM
01:00 PM
01:30 PM
02:00 PM
02:30 PM
03:00 PM
03:30 PM
04:00 PM
04:30 PM
05:00 PM
05:30 PM
06:00 PM
06:30 PM
07:00 PM
07:30 PM
08:00 PM
08:30 PM

FRIDAY 30

Good Friday
Passover Begins

07:00 AM
07:30 AM
08:00 AM
08:30 AM
09:00 AM
09:30 AM
10:00 AM
10:30 AM
11:00 AM
11:30 AM
12:00 PM
12:30 PM
01:00 PM
01:30 PM
02:00 PM
02:30 PM
03:00 PM
03:30 PM
04:00 PM
04:30 PM
05:00 PM
05:30 PM
06:00 PM
06:30 PM
07:00 PM
07:30 PM
08:00 PM
08:30 PM

SATURDAY 31

SUNDAY 1

Easter Sunday

MARCH

FEBRUARY 2018						
S	M	T	W	T	F	S
				1	2	3
4	5	6	7	8	9	10
11	12	13	14	15	16	17
18	19	20	21	22	23	24
25	26	27	28			

MARCH 2018						
S	M	T	W	T	F	S
				1	2	3
4	5	6	7	8	9	10
11	12	13	14	15	16	17
18	19	20	21	22	23	24
25	26	27	28	29	30	31

APRIL 2018						
S	M	T	W	T	F	S
1	2	3	4	5	6	7
8	9	10	11	12	13	14
15	16	17	18	19	20	21
22	23	24	25	26	27	28
29	30					

Prayer Requests

REFLECTIONS

I can do everything through Christ, who gives me strength.

Philippians 4:13 NLT

NOTES

To Do

- [ ]
- [ ]
- [ ]
- [ ]
- [ ]
- [ ]
- [ ]
- [ ]
- [ ]
- [ ]
- [ ]
- [ ]
- [ ]
- [ ]
- [ ]

APRIL

2018

I will sing of the Lord's great love forever;
with my mouth I will make your faithfulness
known through all generations.
I will declare that your
love stands firm forever,
that you have established
your faithfulness in heaven itself.

PSALM 89:1-2 NIV

MY GOALS FOR THE MONTH

_____
_____
_____
_____
_____
_____
_____
_____
_____
_____
_____
_____
_____
_____
_____
_____
_____
_____
_____
_____

MONTH AT A GLANCE

SUNDAY	1
MONDAY	2
TUESDAY	3
WEDNESDAY	4
THURSDAY	5
FRIDAY	6
SATURDAY	7
SUNDAY	8
MONDAY	9
TUESDAY	10
WEDNESDAY	11
THURSDAY	12
FRIDAY	13
SATURDAY	14
SUNDAY	15
MONDAY	16
TUESDAY	17
WEDNESDAY	18
THURSDAY	19
FRIDAY	20
SATURDAY	21
SUNDAY	22
MONDAY	23
TUESDAY	24
WEDNESDAY	25
THURSDAY	26
FRIDAY	27
SATURDAY	28
SUNDAY	29
MONDAY	30

APRIL

> *The LORD will be your confidence,*
> *And will keep your foot from being caught.*
>
> Proverbs 3:26 NKJV

MONDAY 2

07:00 AM
07:30 AM
08:00 AM
08:30 AM
09:00 AM
09:30 AM
10:00 AM
10:30 AM
11:00 AM
11:30 AM
12:00 PM
12:30 PM
01:00 PM
01:30 PM
02:00 PM
02:30 PM
03:00 PM
03:30 PM
04:00 PM
04:30 PM
05:00 PM
05:30 PM
06:00 PM
06:30 PM
07:00 PM
07:30 PM
08:00 PM
08:30 PM

TUESDAY 3

07:00 AM
07:30 AM
08:00 AM
08:30 AM
09:00 AM
09:30 AM
10:00 AM
10:30 AM
11:00 AM
11:30 AM
12:00 PM
12:30 PM
01:00 PM
01:30 PM
02:00 PM
02:30 PM
03:00 PM
03:30 PM
04:00 PM
04:30 PM
05:00 PM
05:30 PM
06:00 PM
06:30 PM
07:00 PM
07:30 PM
08:00 PM
08:30 PM

WEDNESDAY 4

07:00 AM
07:30 AM
08:00 AM
08:30 AM
09:00 AM
09:30 AM
10:00 AM
10:30 AM
11:00 AM
11:30 AM
12:00 PM
12:30 PM
01:00 PM
01:30 PM
02:00 PM
02:30 PM
03:00 PM
03:30 PM
04:00 PM
04:30 PM
05:00 PM
05:30 PM
06:00 PM
06:30 PM
07:00 PM
07:30 PM
08:00 PM
08:30 PM

MARCH 2018

S	M	T	W	T	F	S
				1	2	3
4	5	6	7	8	9	10
11	12	13	14	15	16	17
18	19	20	21	22	23	24
25	26	27	28	29	30	31

APRIL 2018

S	M	T	W	T	F	S
1	2	3	4	5	6	7
8	9	10	11	12	13	14
15	16	17	18	19	20	21
22	23	24	25	26	27	28
29	30					

MAY 2018

S	M	T	W	T	F	S
		1	2	3	4	5
6	7	8	9	10	11	12
13	14	15	16	17	18	19
20	21	22	23	24	25	26
27	28	29	30	31		

THURSDAY 5

07:00 AM	
07:30 AM	
08:00 AM	
08:30 AM	
09:00 AM	
09:30 AM	
10:00 AM	
10:30 AM	
11:00 AM	
11:30 AM	
12:00 PM	
12:30 PM	
01:00 PM	
01:30 PM	
02:00 PM	
02:30 PM	
03:00 PM	
03:30 PM	
04:00 PM	
04:30 PM	
05:00 PM	
05:30 PM	
06:00 PM	
06:30 PM	
07:00 PM	
07:30 PM	
08:00 PM	
08:30 PM	

FRIDAY 6

07:00 AM	
07:30 AM	
08:00 AM	
08:30 AM	
09:00 AM	
09:30 AM	
10:00 AM	
10:30 AM	
11:00 AM	
11:30 AM	
12:00 PM	
12:30 PM	
01:00 PM	
01:30 PM	
02:00 PM	
02:30 PM	
03:00 PM	
03:30 PM	
04:00 PM	
04:30 PM	
05:00 PM	
05:30 PM	
06:00 PM	
06:30 PM	
07:00 PM	
07:30 PM	
08:00 PM	
08:30 PM	

SATURDAY 7

Passover Ends

SUNDAY 8

APRIL

MARCH 2018
S M T W T F S
            1 2 3
4 5 6 7 8 9 10
11 12 13 14 15 16 17
18 19 20 21 22 23 24
25 26 27 28 29 30 31

APRIL 2018
S M T W T F S
1 2 3 4 5 6 7
8 9 10 11 12 13 14
15 16 17 18 19 20 21
22 23 24 25 26 27 28
29 30

MAY 2018
S M T W T F S
      1 2 3 4 5
6 7 8 9 10 11 12
13 14 15 16 17 18 19
20 21 22 23 24 25 26
27 28 29 30 31

A P R

Prayer Requests

_____
_____
_____
_____
_____
_____
_____
_____
_____
_____

REFLECTIONS

*Let us then
approach God's
throne of grace
with confidence,
so that we may
receive mercy
and find grace
to help us in our
time of need.*

Hebrews 4:16 NIV

_____
_____
_____
_____
_____
_____
_____
_____
_____
_____
_____
_____
_____
_____

NOTES

To Do

- [ ]
- [ ]
- [ ]
- [ ]
- [ ]
- [ ]
- [ ]
- [ ]
- [ ]
- [ ]
- [ ]
- [ ]
- [ ]
- [ ]
- [ ]

APRIL

APR

MONDAY 9	TUESDAY 10 — First Day of Passover	WEDNESDAY 11
07:00 AM	07:00 AM	07:00 AM
07:30 AM	07:30 AM	07:30 AM
08:00 AM	08:00 AM	08:00 AM
08:30 AM	08:30 AM	08:30 AM
09:00 AM	09:00 AM	09:00 AM
09:30 AM	09:30 AM	09:30 AM
10:00 AM	10:00 AM	10:00 AM
10:30 AM	10:30 AM	10:30 AM
11:00 AM	11:00 AM	11:00 AM
11:30 AM	11:30 AM	11:30 AM
12:00 PM	12:00 PM	12:00 PM
12:30 PM	12:30 PM	12:30 PM
01:00 PM	01:00 PM	01:00 PM
01:30 PM	01:30 PM	01:30 PM
02:00 PM	02:00 PM	02:00 PM
02:30 PM	02:30 PM	02:30 PM
03:00 PM	03:00 PM	03:00 PM
03:30 PM	03:30 PM	03:30 PM
04:00 PM	04:00 PM	04:00 PM
04:30 PM	04:30 PM	04:30 PM
05:00 PM	05:00 PM	05:00 PM
05:30 PM	05:30 PM	05:30 PM
06:00 PM	06:00 PM	06:00 PM
06:30 PM	06:30 PM	06:30 PM
07:00 PM	07:00 PM	07:00 PM
07:30 PM	07:30 PM	07:30 PM
08:00 PM	08:00 PM	08:00 PM
08:30 PM	08:30 PM	08:30 PM

MARCH 2018
S	M	T	W	T	F	S
				1	2	3
4	5	6	7	8	9	10
11	12	13	14	15	16	17
18	19	20	21	22	23	24
25	26	27	28	29	30	31

APRIL 2018
S	M	T	W	T	F	S
1	2	3	4	5	6	7
8	9	10	11	12	13	14
15	16	17	18	19	20	21
22	23	24	25	26	27	28
29	30					

MAY 2018
S	M	T	W	T	F	S
		1	2	3	4	5
6	7	8	9	10	11	12
13	14	15	16	17	18	19
20	21	22	23	24	25	26
27	28	29	30	31		

APRIL

APR

THURSDAY 12

07:00 AM	
07:30 AM	
08:00 AM	
08:30 AM	
09:00 AM	
09:30 AM	
10:00 AM	
10:30 AM	
11:00 AM	
11:30 AM	
12:00 PM	
12:30 PM	
01:00 PM	
01:30 PM	
02:00 PM	
02:30 PM	
03:00 PM	
03:30 PM	
04:00 PM	
04:30 PM	
05:00 PM	
05:30 PM	
06:00 PM	
06:30 PM	
07:00 PM	
07:30 PM	
08:00 PM	
08:30 PM	

FRIDAY 13 — Good Friday

07:00 AM	
07:30 AM	
08:00 AM	
08:30 AM	
09:00 AM	
09:30 AM	
10:00 AM	
10:30 AM	
11:00 AM	
11:30 AM	
12:00 PM	
12:30 PM	
01:00 PM	
01:30 PM	
02:00 PM	
02:30 PM	
03:00 PM	
03:30 PM	
04:00 PM	
04:30 PM	
05:00 PM	
05:30 PM	
06:00 PM	
06:30 PM	
07:00 PM	
07:30 PM	
08:00 PM	
08:30 PM	

SATURDAY 14

SUNDAY 15 — Easter Sunday

APRIL

MARCH 2018
S M T W T F S
1 2 3
4 5 6 7 8 9 10
11 12 13 14 15 16 17
18 19 20 21 22 23 24
25 26 27 28 29 30 31

APRIL 2018
S M T W T F S
1 2 3 4 5 6 7
8 9 10 11 12 13 14
15 16 17 18 19 20 21
22 23 24 25 26 27 28
29 30

MAY 2018
S M T W T F S
1 2 3 4 5
6 7 8 9 10 11 12
13 14 15 16 17 18 19
20 21 22 23 24 25 26
27 28 29 30 31

APR

Prayer Requests

REFLECTIONS

We are God's masterpiece. He has created us anew in Christ Jesus, so we can do the good things he planned for us long ago.

Ephesians 2:10 NLT

NOTES

To Do

APRIL

APR

MONDAY 16	TUESDAY 17 Last Day of Passover	WEDNESDAY 18
07:00 AM	07:00 AM	07:00 AM
07:30 AM	07:30 AM	07:30 AM
08:00 AM	08:00 AM	08:00 AM
08:30 AM	08:30 AM	08:30 AM
09:00 AM	09:00 AM	09:00 AM
09:30 AM	09:30 AM	09:30 AM
10:00 AM	10:00 AM	10:00 AM
10:30 AM	10:30 AM	10:30 AM
11:00 AM	11:00 AM	11:00 AM
11:30 AM	11:30 AM	11:30 AM
12:00 PM	12:00 PM	12:00 PM
12:30 PM	12:30 PM	12:30 PM
01:00 PM	01:00 PM	01:00 PM
01:30 PM	01:30 PM	01:30 PM
02:00 PM	02:00 PM	02:00 PM
02:30 PM	02:30 PM	02:30 PM
03:00 PM	03:00 PM	03:00 PM
03:30 PM	03:30 PM	03:30 PM
04:00 PM	04:00 PM	04:00 PM
04:30 PM	04:30 PM	04:30 PM
05:00 PM	05:00 PM	05:00 PM
05:30 PM	05:30 PM	05:30 PM
06:00 PM	06:00 PM	06:00 PM
06:30 PM	06:30 PM	06:30 PM
07:00 PM	07:00 PM	07:00 PM
07:30 PM	07:30 PM	07:30 PM
08:00 PM	08:00 PM	08:00 PM
08:30 PM	08:30 PM	08:30 PM

MARCH 2018
S	M	T	W	T	F	S
				1	2	3
4	5	6	7	8	9	10
11	12	13	14	15	16	17
18	19	20	21	22	23	24
25	26	27	28	29	30	31

APRIL 2018
S	M	T	W	T	F	S
1	2	3	4	5	6	7
8	9	10	11	12	13	14
15	16	17	18	19	20	21
22	23	24	25	26	27	28
29	30					

MAY 2018
S	M	T	W	T	F	S
		1	2	3	4	5
6	7	8	9	10	11	12
13	14	15	16	17	18	19
20	21	22	23	24	25	26
27	28	29	30	31		

APRIL

APR

THURSDAY 19

- 07:00 AM
- 07:30 AM
- 08:00 AM
- 08:30 AM
- 09:00 AM
- 09:30 AM
- 10:00 AM
- 10:30 AM
- 11:00 AM
- 11:30 AM
- 12:00 PM
- 12:30 PM
- 01:00 PM
- 01:30 PM
- 02:00 PM
- 02:30 PM
- 03:00 PM
- 03:30 PM
- 04:00 PM
- 04:30 PM
- 05:00 PM
- 05:30 PM
- 06:00 PM
- 06:30 PM
- 07:00 PM
- 07:30 PM
- 08:00 PM
- 08:30 PM

FRIDAY 20

- 07:00 AM
- 07:30 AM
- 08:00 AM
- 08:30 AM
- 09:00 AM
- 09:30 AM
- 10:00 AM
- 10:30 AM
- 11:00 AM
- 11:30 AM
- 12:00 PM
- 12:30 PM
- 01:00 PM
- 01:30 PM
- 02:00 PM
- 02:30 PM
- 03:00 PM
- 03:30 PM
- 04:00 PM
- 04:30 PM
- 05:00 PM
- 05:30 PM
- 06:00 PM
- 06:30 PM
- 07:00 PM
- 07:30 PM
- 08:00 PM
- 08:30 PM

SATURDAY 21

SUNDAY 22

APRIL

MARCH 2018
S M T W T F S
1 2 3
4 5 6 7 8 9 10
11 12 13 14 15 16 17
18 19 20 21 22 23 24
25 26 27 28 29 30 31

APRIL 2018
S M T W T F S
1 2 3 4 5 6 7
8 9 10 11 12 13 14
15 16 17 18 19 20 21
22 23 24 25 26 27 28
29 30

MAY 2018
S M T W T F S
1 2 3 4 5
6 7 8 9 10 11 12
13 14 15 16 17 18 19
20 21 22 23 24 25 26
27 28 29 30 31

APR

Prayer Requests

REFLECTIONS

Be of the same mind toward one another. Do not set your mind on high things, but associate with the humble. Do not be wise in your own opinion.

Romans 12:16 NKJV

NOTES

To Do

APR

APRIL

APR

MONDAY 23	TUESDAY 24	WEDNESDAY 25
07:00 AM	07:00 AM	07:00 AM
07:30 AM	07:30 AM	07:30 AM
08:00 AM	08:00 AM	08:00 AM
08:30 AM	08:30 AM	08:30 AM
09:00 AM	09:00 AM	09:00 AM
09:30 AM	09:30 AM	09:30 AM
10:00 AM	10:00 AM	10:00 AM
10:30 AM	10:30 AM	10:30 AM
11:00 AM	11:00 AM	11:00 AM
11:30 AM	11:30 AM	11:30 AM
12:00 PM	12:00 PM	12:00 PM
12:30 PM	12:30 PM	12:30 PM
01:00 PM	01:00 PM	01:00 PM
01:30 PM	01:30 PM	01:30 PM
02:00 PM	02:00 PM	02:00 PM
02:30 PM	02:30 PM	02:30 PM
03:00 PM	03:00 PM	03:00 PM
03:30 PM	03:30 PM	03:30 PM
04:00 PM	04:00 PM	04:00 PM
04:30 PM	04:30 PM	04:30 PM
05:00 PM	05:00 PM	05:00 PM
05:30 PM	05:30 PM	05:30 PM
06:00 PM	06:00 PM	06:00 PM
06:30 PM	06:30 PM	06:30 PM
07:00 PM	07:00 PM	07:00 PM
07:30 PM	07:30 PM	07:30 PM
08:00 PM	08:00 PM	08:00 PM
08:30 PM	08:30 PM	08:30 PM

MARCH 2018						
S	M	T	W	T	F	S
				1	2	3
4	5	6	7	8	9	10
11	12	13	14	15	16	17
18	19	20	21	22	23	24
25	26	27	28	29	30	31

APRIL 2018						
S	M	T	W	T	F	S
1	2	3	4	5	6	7
8	9	10	11	12	13	14
15	16	17	18	19	20	21
22	23	24	25	26	27	28
29	30					

MAY 2018						
S	M	T	W	T	F	S
		1	2	3	4	5
6	7	8	9	10	11	12
13	14	15	16	17	18	19
20	21	22	23	24	25	26
27	28	29	30	31		

APRIL

APR

THURSDAY 26

07:00 AM
07:30 AM
08:00 AM
08:30 AM
09:00 AM
09:30 AM
10:00 AM
10:30 AM
11:00 AM
11:30 AM
12:00 PM
12:30 PM
01:00 PM
01:30 PM
02:00 PM
02:30 PM
03:00 PM
03:30 PM
04:00 PM
04:30 PM
05:00 PM
05:30 PM
06:00 PM
06:30 PM
07:00 PM
07:30 PM
08:00 PM
08:30 PM

FRIDAY 27

07:00 AM
07:30 AM
08:00 AM
08:30 AM
09:00 AM
09:30 AM
10:00 AM
10:30 AM
11:00 AM
11:30 AM
12:00 PM
12:30 PM
01:00 PM
01:30 PM
02:00 PM
02:30 PM
03:00 PM
03:30 PM
04:00 PM
04:30 PM
05:00 PM
05:30 PM
06:00 PM
06:30 PM
07:00 PM
07:30 PM
08:00 PM
08:30 PM

SATURDAY 28

SUNDAY 29

APRIL

MARCH 2018
S M T W T F S
1 2 3
4 5 6 7 8 9 10
11 12 13 14 15 16 17
18 19 20 21 22 23 24
25 26 27 28 29 30 31

APRIL 2018
S M T W T F S
1 2 3 4 5 6 7
8 9 10 11 12 13 14
15 16 17 18 19 20 21
22 23 24 25 26 27 28
29 30

MAY 2018
S M T W T F S
1 2 3 4 5
6 7 8 9 10 11 12
13 14 15 16 17 18 19
20 21 22 23 24 25 26
27 28 29 30 31

APR

Prayer Requests

REFLECTIONS

*Be strong and
courageous. Do
not be frightened,
and do not be
dismayed, for
the Lord your
God is with you
wherever you go.*

Joshua 1:9 ESV

NOTES

_____
_____
_____
_____
_____
_____
_____
_____
_____
_____
_____
_____
_____
_____
_____
_____
_____
_____

To Do

- [ ] _____
- [ ] _____
- [ ] _____
- [ ] _____
- [ ] _____
- [ ] _____
- [ ] _____
- [ ] _____
- [ ] _____
- [ ] _____
- [ ] _____
- [ ] _____
- [ ] _____
- [ ] _____

MAY

2018

Be my rock of refuge,
to which I can always go;
give the command to save me,
for you are my rock
and my fortress....
You have been my hope,
Sovereign LORD,
my confidence since my youth.

PSALM 71:3, 5 NIV

MY GOALS FOR THE MONTH

MONTH AT A GLANCE

TUESDAY	1	
WEDNESDAY	2	
THURSDAY	3	
FRIDAY	4	
SATURDAY	5	
SUNDAY	6	
MONDAY	7	
TUESDAY	8	
WEDNESDAY	9	
THURSDAY	10	
FRIDAY	11	
SATURDAY	12	
SUNDAY	13	
MONDAY	14	
TUESDAY	15	
WEDNESDAY	16	
THURSDAY	17	
FRIDAY	18	
SATURDAY	19	
SUNDAY	20	
MONDAY	21	
TUESDAY	22	
WEDNESDAY	23	
THURSDAY	24	
FRIDAY	25	
SATURDAY	26	
SUNDAY	27	
MONDAY	28	
TUESDAY	29	
WEDNESDAY	30	
THURSDAY	31	

MAY

> The heavens are telling of the glory of God;
> And their expanse is declaring the work of His hands.
>
> Psalm 19:1 NASB

MONDAY 30	TUESDAY 1	WEDNESDAY 2
07:00 AM	07:00 AM	07:00 AM
07:30 AM	07:30 AM	07:30 AM
08:00 AM	08:00 AM	08:00 AM
08:30 AM	08:30 AM	08:30 AM
09:00 AM	09:00 AM	09:00 AM
09:30 AM	09:30 AM	09:30 AM
10:00 AM	10:00 AM	10:00 AM
10:30 AM	10:30 AM	10:30 AM
11:00 AM	11:00 AM	11:00 AM
11:30 AM	11:30 AM	11:30 AM
12:00 PM	12:00 PM	12:00 PM
12:30 PM	12:30 PM	12:30 PM
01:00 PM	01:00 PM	01:00 PM
01:30 PM	01:30 PM	01:30 PM
02:00 PM	02:00 PM	02:00 PM
02:30 PM	02:30 PM	02:30 PM
03:00 PM	03:00 PM	03:00 PM
03:30 PM	03:30 PM	03:30 PM
04:00 PM	04:00 PM	04:00 PM
04:30 PM	04:30 PM	04:30 PM
05:00 PM	05:00 PM	05:00 PM
05:30 PM	05:30 PM	05:30 PM
06:00 PM	06:00 PM	06:00 PM
06:30 PM	06:30 PM	06:30 PM
07:00 PM	07:00 PM	07:00 PM
07:30 PM	07:30 PM	07:30 PM
08:00 PM	08:00 PM	08:00 PM
08:30 PM	08:30 PM	08:30 PM

APRIL 2018	MAY 2018	JUNE 2018
S M T W T F S	S M T W T F S	S M T W T F S
1 2 3 4 5 6 7	1 2 3 4 5	1 2
8 9 10 11 12 13 14	6 7 8 9 10 11 12	3 4 5 6 7 8 9
15 16 17 18 19 20 21	13 14 15 16 17 18 19	10 11 12 13 14 15 16
22 23 24 25 26 27 28	20 21 22 23 24 25 26	17 18 19 20 21 22 23
29 30	27 28 29 30 31	24 25 26 27 28 29 30

MAY

MAY

THURSDAY 3 — National Day of Prayer

07:00 AM
07:30 AM
08:00 AM
08:30 AM
09:00 AM
09:30 AM
10:00 AM
10:30 AM
11:00 AM
11:30 AM
12:00 PM
12:30 PM
01:00 PM
01:30 PM
02:00 PM
02:30 PM
03:00 PM
03:30 PM
04:00 PM
04:30 PM
05:00 PM
05:30 PM
06:00 PM
06:30 PM
07:00 PM
07:30 PM
08:00 PM
08:30 PM

FRIDAY 4

07:00 AM
07:30 AM
08:00 AM
08:30 AM
09:00 AM
09:30 AM
10:00 AM
10:30 AM
11:00 AM
11:30 AM
12:00 PM
12:30 PM
01:00 PM
01:30 PM
02:00 PM
02:30 PM
03:00 PM
03:30 PM
04:00 PM
04:30 PM
05:00 PM
05:30 PM
06:00 PM
06:30 PM
07:00 PM
07:30 PM
08:00 PM
08:30 PM

SATURDAY 5

SUNDAY 6

MAY

APRIL 2018						
S	M	T	W	T	F	S
1	2	3	4	5	6	7
8	9	10	11	12	13	14
15	16	17	18	19	20	21
22	23	24	25	26	27	28
29	30					

MAY 2018						
S	M	T	W	T	F	S
		1	2	3	4	5
6	7	8	9	10	11	12
13	14	15	16	17	18	19
20	21	22	23	24	25	26
27	28	29	30	31		

JUNE 2018						
S	M	T	W	T	F	S
					1	2
3	4	5	6	7	8	9
10	11	12	13	14	15	16
17	18	19	20	21	22	23
24	25	26	27	28	29	30

Prayer Requests

REFLECTIONS

*The whole
earth is filled
with awe at
your wonders.*

Psalm 65:8 NIV

NOTES

To Do

MAY

MONDAY 7	TUESDAY 8	WEDNESDAY 9
07:00 AM	07:00 AM	07:00 AM
07:30 AM	07:30 AM	07:30 AM
08:00 AM	08:00 AM	08:00 AM
08:30 AM	08:30 AM	08:30 AM
09:00 AM	09:00 AM	09:00 AM
09:30 AM	09:30 AM	09:30 AM
10:00 AM	10:00 AM	10:00 AM
10:30 AM	10:30 AM	10:30 AM
11:00 AM	11:00 AM	11:00 AM
11:30 AM	11:30 AM	11:30 AM
12:00 PM	12:00 PM	12:00 PM
12:30 PM	12:30 PM	12:30 PM
01:00 PM	01:00 PM	01:00 PM
01:30 PM	01:30 PM	01:30 PM
02:00 PM	02:00 PM	02:00 PM
02:30 PM	02:30 PM	02:30 PM
03:00 PM	03:00 PM	03:00 PM
03:30 PM	03:30 PM	03:30 PM
04:00 PM	04:00 PM	04:00 PM
04:30 PM	04:30 PM	04:30 PM
05:00 PM	05:00 PM	05:00 PM
05:30 PM	05:30 PM	05:30 PM
06:00 PM	06:00 PM	06:00 PM
06:30 PM	06:30 PM	06:30 PM
07:00 PM	07:00 PM	07:00 PM
07:30 PM	07:30 PM	07:30 PM
08:00 PM	08:00 PM	08:00 PM
08:30 PM	08:30 PM	08:30 PM

APRIL 2018	MAY 2018	JUNE 2018
S M T W T F S	S M T W T F S	S M T W T F S
1 2 3 4 5 6 7	1 2 3 4 5	1 2
8 9 10 11 12 13 14	6 7 8 9 10 11 12	3 4 5 6 7 8 9
15 16 17 18 19 20 21	13 14 15 16 17 18 19	10 11 12 13 14 15 16
22 23 24 25 26 27 28	20 21 22 23 24 25 26	17 18 19 20 21 22 23
29 30	27 28 29 30 31	24 25 26 27 28 29 30

MAY

MAY

THURSDAY 10

- 07:00 AM
- 07:30 AM
- 08:00 AM
- 08:30 AM
- 09:00 AM
- 09:30 AM
- 10:00 AM
- 10:30 AM
- 11:00 AM
- 11:30 AM
- 12:00 PM
- 12:30 PM
- 01:00 PM
- 01:30 PM
- 02:00 PM
- 02:30 PM
- 03:00 PM
- 03:30 PM
- 04:00 PM
- 04:30 PM
- 05:00 PM
- 05:30 PM
- 06:00 PM
- 06:30 PM
- 07:00 PM
- 07:30 PM
- 08:00 PM
- 08:30 PM

FRIDAY 11

- 07:00 AM
- 07:30 AM
- 08:00 AM
- 08:30 AM
- 09:00 AM
- 09:30 AM
- 10:00 AM
- 10:30 AM
- 11:00 AM
- 11:30 AM
- 12:00 PM
- 12:30 PM
- 01:00 PM
- 01:30 PM
- 02:00 PM
- 02:30 PM
- 03:00 PM
- 03:30 PM
- 04:00 PM
- 04:30 PM
- 05:00 PM
- 05:30 PM
- 06:00 PM
- 06:30 PM
- 07:00 PM
- 07:30 PM
- 08:00 PM
- 08:30 PM

SATURDAY 12

SUNDAY 13

Mother's Day

MAY

APRIL 2018

S	M	T	W	T	F	S
1	2	3	4	5	6	7
8	9	10	11	12	13	14
15	16	17	18	19	20	21
22	23	24	25	26	27	28
29	30					

MAY 2018

S	M	T	W	T	F	S
		1	2	3	4	5
6	7	8	9	10	11	12
13	14	15	16	17	18	19
20	21	22	23	24	25	26
27	28	29	30	31		

JUNE 2018

S	M	T	W	T	F	S
					1	2
3	4	5	6	7	8	9
10	11	12	13	14	15	16
17	18	19	20	21	22	23
24	25	26	27	28	29	30

Prayer Requests

REFLECTIONS

Why am I so sad?
Why am I so upset?
I should put my
hope in God
and keep
praising him.

Psalm 42:11 NCV

NOTES

To Do

MAY

MONDAY 14	TUESDAY 15	WEDNESDAY 16
07:00 AM	07:00 AM	07:00 AM
07:30 AM	07:30 AM	07:30 AM
08:00 AM	08:00 AM	08:00 AM
08:30 AM	08:30 AM	08:30 AM
09:00 AM	09:00 AM	09:00 AM
09:30 AM	09:30 AM	09:30 AM
10:00 AM	10:00 AM	10:00 AM
10:30 AM	10:30 AM	10:30 AM
11:00 AM	11:00 AM	11:00 AM
11:30 AM	11:30 AM	11:30 AM
12:00 PM	12:00 PM	12:00 PM
12:30 PM	12:30 PM	12:30 PM
01:00 PM	01:00 PM	01:00 PM
01:30 PM	01:30 PM	01:30 PM
02:00 PM	02:00 PM	02:00 PM
02:30 PM	02:30 PM	02:30 PM
03:00 PM	03:00 PM	03:00 PM
03:30 PM	03:30 PM	03:30 PM
04:00 PM	04:00 PM	04:00 PM
04:30 PM	04:30 PM	04:30 PM
05:00 PM	05:00 PM	05:00 PM
05:30 PM	05:30 PM	05:30 PM
06:00 PM	06:00 PM	06:00 PM
06:30 PM	06:30 PM	06:30 PM
07:00 PM	07:00 PM	07:00 PM
07:30 PM	07:30 PM	07:30 PM
08:00 PM	08:00 PM	08:00 PM
08:30 PM	08:30 PM	08:30 PM

APRIL 2018
S M T W T F S
1 2 3 4 5 6 7
8 9 10 11 12 13 14
15 16 17 18 19 20 21
22 23 24 25 26 27 28
29 30

MAY 2018
S M T W T F S
1 2 3 4 5
6 7 8 9 10 11 12
13 14 15 16 17 18 19
20 21 22 23 24 25 26
27 28 29 30 31

JUNE 2018
S M T W T F S
1 2
3 4 5 6 7 8 9
10 11 12 13 14 15 16
17 18 19 20 21 22 23
24 25 26 27 28 29 30

MAY

MAY

THURSDAY 17

- 07:00 AM
- 07:30 AM
- 08:00 AM
- 08:30 AM
- 09:00 AM
- 09:30 AM
- 10:00 AM
- 10:30 AM
- 11:00 AM
- 11:30 AM
- 12:00 PM
- 12:30 PM
- 01:00 PM
- 01:30 PM
- 02:00 PM
- 02:30 PM
- 03:00 PM
- 03:30 PM
- 04:00 PM
- 04:30 PM
- 05:00 PM
- 05:30 PM
- 06:00 PM
- 06:30 PM
- 07:00 PM
- 07:30 PM
- 08:00 PM
- 08:30 PM

FRIDAY 18

- 07:00 AM
- 07:30 AM
- 08:00 AM
- 08:30 AM
- 09:00 AM
- 09:30 AM
- 10:00 AM
- 10:30 AM
- 11:00 AM
- 11:30 AM
- 12:00 PM
- 12:30 PM
- 01:00 PM
- 01:30 PM
- 02:00 PM
- 02:30 PM
- 03:00 PM
- 03:30 PM
- 04:00 PM
- 04:30 PM
- 05:00 PM
- 05:30 PM
- 06:00 PM
- 06:30 PM
- 07:00 PM
- 07:30 PM
- 08:00 PM
- 08:30 PM

SATURDAY 19

SUNDAY 20

Pentecost

MAY

APRIL 2018
S M T W T F S
1 2 3 4 5 6 7
8 9 10 11 12 13 14
15 16 17 18 19 20 21
22 23 24 25 26 27 28
29 30

MAY 2018
S M T W T F S
1 2 3 4 5
6 7 8 9 10 11 12
13 14 15 16 17 18 19
20 21 22 23 24 25 26
27 28 29 30 31

JUNE 2018
S M T W T F S
1 2
3 4 5 6 7 8 9
10 11 12 13 14 15 16
17 18 19 20 21 22 23
24 25 26 27 28 29 30

Prayer Requests

_____
_____
_____
_____
_____
_____
_____
_____
_____
_____

MAY

REFLECTIONS

Take a new grip with your tired hands and strengthen your weak knees. Mark out a straight path for your feet so that those who are weak and lame will not fall but become strong.

Hebrews 12:12-14
NLT

_____
_____
_____
_____
_____
_____
_____
_____
_____
_____
_____
_____
_____

NOTES

To Do

- [ ]
- [ ]
- [ ]
- [ ]
- [ ]
- [ ]
- [ ]
- [ ]
- [ ]
- [ ]
- [ ]
- [ ]
- [ ]
- [ ]

MAY

MONDAY 21	TUESDAY 22	WEDNESDAY 23
07:00 AM	07:00 AM	07:00 AM
07:30 AM	07:30 AM	07:30 AM
08:00 AM	08:00 AM	08:00 AM
08:30 AM	08:30 AM	08:30 AM
09:00 AM	09:00 AM	09:00 AM
09:30 AM	09:30 AM	09:30 AM
10:00 AM	10:00 AM	10:00 AM
10:30 AM	10:30 AM	10:30 AM
11:00 AM	11:00 AM	11:00 AM
11:30 AM	11:30 AM	11:30 AM
12:00 PM	12:00 PM	12:00 PM
12:30 PM	12:30 PM	12:30 PM
01:00 PM	01:00 PM	01:00 PM
01:30 PM	01:30 PM	01:30 PM
02:00 PM	02:00 PM	02:00 PM
02:30 PM	02:30 PM	02:30 PM
03:00 PM	03:00 PM	03:00 PM
03:30 PM	03:30 PM	03:30 PM
04:00 PM	04:00 PM	04:00 PM
04:30 PM	04:30 PM	04:30 PM
05:00 PM	05:00 PM	05:00 PM
05:30 PM	05:30 PM	05:30 PM
06:00 PM	06:00 PM	06:00 PM
06:30 PM	06:30 PM	06:30 PM
07:00 PM	07:00 PM	07:00 PM
07:30 PM	07:30 PM	07:30 PM
08:00 PM	08:00 PM	08:00 PM
08:30 PM	08:30 PM	08:30 PM

APRIL 2018
S M T W T F S
1 2 3 4 5 6 7
8 9 10 11 12 13 14
15 16 17 18 19 20 21
22 23 24 25 26 27 28
29 30

MAY 2018
S M T W T F S
1 2 3 4 5
6 7 8 9 10 11 12
13 14 15 16 17 18 19
20 21 22 23 24 25 26
27 28 29 30 31

JUNE 2018
S M T W T F S
1 2
3 4 5 6 7 8 9
10 11 12 13 14 15 16
17 18 19 20 21 22 23
24 25 26 27 28 29 30

MAY

M A Y

THURSDAY 24

07:00 AM	
07:30 AM	
08:00 AM	
08:30 AM	
09:00 AM	
09:30 AM	
10:00 AM	
10:30 AM	
11:00 AM	
11:30 AM	
12:00 PM	
12:30 PM	
01:00 PM	
01:30 PM	
02:00 PM	
02:30 PM	
03:00 PM	
03:30 PM	
04:00 PM	
04:30 PM	
05:00 PM	
05:30 PM	
06:00 PM	
06:30 PM	
07:00 PM	
07:30 PM	
08:00 PM	
08:30 PM	

FRIDAY 25

07:00 AM	
07:30 AM	
08:00 AM	
08:30 AM	
09:00 AM	
09:30 AM	
10:00 AM	
10:30 AM	
11:00 AM	
11:30 AM	
12:00 PM	
12:30 PM	
01:00 PM	
01:30 PM	
02:00 PM	
02:30 PM	
03:00 PM	
03:30 PM	
04:00 PM	
04:30 PM	
05:00 PM	
05:30 PM	
06:00 PM	
06:30 PM	
07:00 PM	
07:30 PM	
08:00 PM	
08:30 PM	

SATURDAY 26

SUNDAY 27

MAY

MAY

APRIL 2018

S	M	T	W	T	F	S
1	2	3	4	5	6	7
8	9	10	11	12	13	14
15	16	17	18	19	20	21
22	23	24	25	26	27	28
29	30					

MAY 2018

S	M	T	W	T	F	S
		1	2	3	4	5
6	7	8	9	10	11	12
13	14	15	16	17	18	19
20	21	22	23	24	25	26
27	28	29	30	31		

JUNE 2018

S	M	T	W	T	F	S
					1	2
3	4	5	6	7	8	9
10	11	12	13	14	15	16
17	18	19	20	21	22	23
24	25	26	27	28	29	30

Prayer Requests

REFLECTIONS

Let us not neglect our meeting together, as some people do, but encourage one another, especially now that the day of his return is drawing near.

Hebrews 10:25 NLT

NOTES

_____

_____

_____

_____

_____

_____

_____

_____

_____

_____

_____

_____

_____

_____

_____

_____

_____

_____

_____

_____

MAY

To Do

- [ ] _____
- [ ] _____
- [ ] _____
- [ ] _____
- [ ] _____
- [ ] _____
- [ ] _____
- [ ] _____
- [ ] _____
- [ ] _____
- [ ] _____
- [ ] _____
- [ ] _____
- [ ] _____
- [ ] _____

MAY

MAY

MONDAY 28 — Memorial Day	TUESDAY 29	WEDNESDAY 30
07:00 AM	07:00 AM	07:00 AM
07:30 AM	07:30 AM	07:30 AM
08:00 AM	08:00 AM	08:00 AM
08:30 AM	08:30 AM	08:30 AM
09:00 AM	09:00 AM	09:00 AM
09:30 AM	09:30 AM	09:30 AM
10:00 AM	10:00 AM	10:00 AM
10:30 AM	10:30 AM	10:30 AM
11:00 AM	11:00 AM	11:00 AM
11:30 AM	11:30 AM	11:30 AM
12:00 PM	12:00 PM	12:00 PM
12:30 PM	12:30 PM	12:30 PM
01:00 PM	01:00 PM	01:00 PM
01:30 PM	01:30 PM	01:30 PM
02:00 PM	02:00 PM	02:00 PM
02:30 PM	02:30 PM	02:30 PM
03:00 PM	03:00 PM	03:00 PM
03:30 PM	03:30 PM	03:30 PM
04:00 PM	04:00 PM	04:00 PM
04:30 PM	04:30 PM	04:30 PM
05:00 PM	05:00 PM	05:00 PM
05:30 PM	05:30 PM	05:30 PM
06:00 PM	06:00 PM	06:00 PM
06:30 PM	06:30 PM	06:30 PM
07:00 PM	07:00 PM	07:00 PM
07:30 PM	07:30 PM	07:30 PM
08:00 PM	08:00 PM	08:00 PM
08:30 PM	08:30 PM	08:30 PM

APRIL 2018						
S	M	T	W	T	F	S
1	2	3	4	5	6	7
8	9	10	11	12	13	14
15	16	17	18	19	20	21
22	23	24	25	26	27	28
29	30					

MAY 2018						
S	M	T	W	T	F	S
		1	2	3	4	5
6	7	8	9	10	11	12
13	14	15	16	17	18	19
20	21	22	23	24	25	26
27	28	29	30	31		

JUNE 2018						
S	M	T	W	T	F	S
					1	2
3	4	5	6	7	8	9
10	11	12	13	14	15	16
17	18	19	20	21	22	23
24	25	26	27	28	29	30

JUNE

THURSDAY 31

07:00 AM
07:30 AM
08:00 AM
08:30 AM
09:00 AM
09:30 AM
10:00 AM
10:30 AM
11:00 AM
11:30 AM
12:00 PM
12:30 PM
01:00 PM
01:30 PM
02:00 PM
02:30 PM
03:00 PM
03:30 PM
04:00 PM
04:30 PM
05:00 PM
05:30 PM
06:00 PM
06:30 PM
07:00 PM
07:30 PM
08:00 PM
08:30 PM

FRIDAY 1

07:00 AM
07:30 AM
08:00 AM
08:30 AM
09:00 AM
09:30 AM
10:00 AM
10:30 AM
11:00 AM
11:30 AM
12:00 PM
12:30 PM
01:00 PM
01:30 PM
02:00 PM
02:30 PM
03:00 PM
03:30 PM
04:00 PM
04:30 PM
05:00 PM
05:30 PM
06:00 PM
06:30 PM
07:00 PM
07:30 PM
08:00 PM
08:30 PM

SATURDAY 2

SUNDAY 3 — Pentecost

MAY

APRIL 2018						
S	M	T	W	T	F	S
1	2	3	4	5	6	7
8	9	10	11	12	13	14
15	16	17	18	19	20	21
22	23	24	25	26	27	28
29	30					

MAY 2018						
S	M	T	W	T	F	S
		1	2	3	4	5
6	7	8	9	10	11	12
13	14	15	16	17	18	19
20	21	22	23	24	25	26
27	28	29	30	31		

JUNE 2018						
S	M	T	W	T	F	S
					1	2
3	4	5	6	7	8	9
10	11	12	13	14	15	16
17	18	19	20	21	22	23
24	25	26	27	28	29	30

Prayer Requests

REFLECTIONS

*Do not let
wisdom and
understanding
out of your sight,
preserve sound
judgment and
discretion;
they will be life
for you.*

Proverbs 3:21-22
NIV

NOTES

_____
_____
_____
_____
_____
_____
_____
_____
_____
_____
_____
_____
_____
_____
_____
_____
_____
_____
_____

To Do

- [ ] _____
- [ ] _____
- [ ] _____
- [ ] _____
- [ ] _____
- [ ] _____
- [ ] _____
- [ ] _____
- [ ] _____
- [ ] _____
- [ ] _____
- [ ] _____
- [ ] _____
- [ ] _____
- [ ] _____

JUNE

2018

> *The LORD your God is in your midst,*
> *a mighty one who will save;*
> *he will rejoice over you with gladness;*
> *he will quiet you by his love;*
> *he will exult over you with loud singing.*
>
> ZEPHANIAH 3:17 ESV

MY GOALS FOR THE MONTH

MONTH AT A GLANCE

FRIDAY	1	
SATURDAY	2	
SUNDAY	3	
MONDAY	4	
TUESDAY	5	
WEDNESDAY	6	
THURSDAY	7	
FRIDAY	8	
SATURDAY	9	
SUNDAY	10	
MONDAY	11	
TUESDAY	12	
WEDNESDAY	13	
THURSDAY	14	
FRIDAY	15	
SATURDAY	16	
SUNDAY	17	
MONDAY	18	
TUESDAY	19	
WEDNESDAY	20	
THURSDAY	21	
FRIDAY	22	
SATURDAY	23	
SUNDAY	24	
MONDAY	25	
TUESDAY	26	
WEDNESDAY	27	
THURSDAY	28	
FRIDAY	29	
SATURDAY	30	

JUNE

MONDAY 4

07:00 AM
07:30 AM
08:00 AM
08:30 AM
09:00 AM
09:30 AM
10:00 AM
10:30 AM
11:00 AM
11:30 AM
12:00 PM
12:30 PM
01:00 PM
01:30 PM
02:00 PM
02:30 PM
03:00 PM
03:30 PM
04:00 PM
04:30 PM
05:00 PM
05:30 PM
06:00 PM
06:30 PM
07:00 PM
07:30 PM
08:00 PM
08:30 PM

TUESDAY 5

07:00 AM
07:30 AM
08:00 AM
08:30 AM
09:00 AM
09:30 AM
10:00 AM
10:30 AM
11:00 AM
11:30 AM
12:00 PM
12:30 PM
01:00 PM
01:30 PM
02:00 PM
02:30 PM
03:00 PM
03:30 PM
04:00 PM
04:30 PM
05:00 PM
05:30 PM
06:00 PM
06:30 PM
07:00 PM
07:30 PM
08:00 PM
08:30 PM

WEDNESDAY 6

07:00 AM
07:30 AM
08:00 AM
08:30 AM
09:00 AM
09:30 AM
10:00 AM
10:30 AM
11:00 AM
11:30 AM
12:00 PM
12:30 PM
01:00 PM
01:30 PM
02:00 PM
02:30 PM
03:00 PM
03:30 PM
04:00 PM
04:30 PM
05:00 PM
05:30 PM
06:00 PM
06:30 PM
07:00 PM
07:30 PM
08:00 PM
08:30 PM

MAY 2018						
S	M	T	W	T	F	S
		1	2	3	4	5
6	7	8	9	10	11	12
13	14	15	16	17	18	19
20	21	22	23	24	25	26
27	28	29	30	31		

JUNE 2018						
S	M	T	W	T	F	S
					1	2
3	4	5	6	7	8	9
10	11	12	13	14	15	16
17	18	19	20	21	22	23
24	25	26	27	28	29	30

JULY 2018						
S	M	T	W	T	F	S
1	2	3	4	5	6	7
8	9	10	11	12	13	14
15	16	17	18	19	20	21
22	23	24	25	26	27	28
29	30	31				

JUNE

THURSDAY 7

07:00 AM
07:30 AM
08:00 AM
08:30 AM
09:00 AM
09:30 AM
10:00 AM
10:30 AM
11:00 AM
11:30 AM
12:00 PM
12:30 PM
01:00 PM
01:30 PM
02:00 PM
02:30 PM
03:00 PM
03:30 PM
04:00 PM
04:30 PM
05:00 PM
05:30 PM
06:00 PM
06:30 PM
07:00 PM
07:30 PM
08:00 PM
08:30 PM

FRIDAY 8

07:00 AM
07:30 AM
08:00 AM
08:30 AM
09:00 AM
09:30 AM
10:00 AM
10:30 AM
11:00 AM
11:30 AM
12:00 PM
12:30 PM
01:00 PM
01:30 PM
02:00 PM
02:30 PM
03:00 PM
03:30 PM
04:00 PM
04:30 PM
05:00 PM
05:30 PM
06:00 PM
06:30 PM
07:00 PM
07:30 PM
08:00 PM
08:30 PM

SATURDAY 9

SUNDAY 10

JUNE

MAY 2018
S	M	T	W	T	F	S
		1	2	3	4	5
6	7	8	9	10	11	12
13	14	15	16	17	18	19
20	21	22	23	24	25	26
27	28	29	30	31		

JUNE 2018
S	M	T	W	T	F	S
					1	2
3	4	5	6	7	8	9
10	11	12	13	14	15	16
17	18	19	20	21	22	23
24	25	26	27	28	29	30

JULY 2018
S	M	T	W	T	F	S
1	2	3	4	5	6	7
8	9	10	11	12	13	14
15	16	17	18	19	20	21
22	23	24	25	26	27	28
29	30	31				

Prayer Requests

JUN

REFLECTIONS

Do your best to present yourself to God as one approved by him, a worker who has no need to be ashamed, rightly explaining the word of truth.

2 Timothy 2:15
NRSV

NOTES

To Do

JUNE

> *Before the mountains were brought forth,*
> *or ever you had formed the earth and the world,*
> *from everlasting to everlasting you are God.*
>
> Psalm 90:2 ESV

MONDAY 11

07:00 AM
07:30 AM
08:00 AM
08:30 AM
09:00 AM
09:30 AM
10:00 AM
10:30 AM
11:00 AM
11:30 AM
12:00 PM
12:30 PM
01:00 PM
01:30 PM
02:00 PM
02:30 PM
03:00 PM
03:30 PM
04:00 PM
04:30 PM
05:00 PM
05:30 PM
06:00 PM
06:30 PM
07:00 PM
07:30 PM
08:00 PM
08:30 PM

TUESDAY 12

07:00 AM
07:30 AM
08:00 AM
08:30 AM
09:00 AM
09:30 AM
10:00 AM
10:30 AM
11:00 AM
11:30 AM
12:00 PM
12:30 PM
01:00 PM
01:30 PM
02:00 PM
02:30 PM
03:00 PM
03:30 PM
04:00 PM
04:30 PM
05:00 PM
05:30 PM
06:00 PM
06:30 PM
07:00 PM
07:30 PM
08:00 PM
08:30 PM

WEDNESDAY 13

07:00 AM
07:30 AM
08:00 AM
08:30 AM
09:00 AM
09:30 AM
10:00 AM
10:30 AM
11:00 AM
11:30 AM
12:00 PM
12:30 PM
01:00 PM
01:30 PM
02:00 PM
02:30 PM
03:00 PM
03:30 PM
04:00 PM
04:30 PM
05:00 PM
05:30 PM
06:00 PM
06:30 PM
07:00 PM
07:30 PM
08:00 PM
08:30 PM

MAY 2018						
S	M	T	W	T	F	S
		1	2	3	4	5
6	7	8	9	10	11	12
13	14	15	16	17	18	19
20	21	22	23	24	25	26
27	28	29	30	31		

JUNE 2018						
S	M	T	W	T	F	S
					1	2
3	4	5	6	7	8	9
10	11	12	13	14	15	16
17	18	19	20	21	22	23
24	25	26	27	28	29	30

JULY 2018						
S	M	T	W	T	F	S
1	2	3	4	5	6	7
8	9	10	11	12	13	14
15	16	17	18	19	20	21
22	23	24	25	26	27	28
29	30	31				

JUNE

THURSDAY 14 — Flag Day

07:00 AM
07:30 AM
08:00 AM
08:30 AM
09:00 AM
09:30 AM
10:00 AM
10:30 AM
11:00 AM
11:30 AM
12:00 PM
12:30 PM
01:00 PM
01:30 PM
02:00 PM
02:30 PM
03:00 PM
03:30 PM
04:00 PM
04:30 PM
05:00 PM
05:30 PM
06:00 PM
06:30 PM
07:00 PM
07:30 PM
08:00 PM
08:30 PM

FRIDAY 15

07:00 AM
07:30 AM
08:00 AM
08:30 AM
09:00 AM
09:30 AM
10:00 AM
10:30 AM
11:00 AM
11:30 AM
12:00 PM
12:30 PM
01:00 PM
01:30 PM
02:00 PM
02:30 PM
03:00 PM
03:30 PM
04:00 PM
04:30 PM
05:00 PM
05:30 PM
06:00 PM
06:30 PM
07:00 PM
07:30 PM
08:00 PM
08:30 PM

SATURDAY 16

SUNDAY 17 — Father's Day

JUN

JUNE

MAY 2018						
S	M	T	W	T	F	S
		1	2	3	4	5
6	7	8	9	10	11	12
13	14	15	16	17	18	19
20	21	22	23	24	25	26
27	28	29	30	31		

JUNE 2018						
S	M	T	W	T	F	S
					1	2
3	4	5	6	7	8	9
10	11	12	13	14	15	16
17	18	19	20	21	22	23
24	25	26	27	28	29	30

JULY 2018						
S	M	T	W	T	F	S
1	2	3	4	5	6	7
8	9	10	11	12	13	14
15	16	17	18	19	20	21
22	23	24	25	26	27	28
29	30	31				

JUN

Prayer Requests

REFLECTIONS

*"I will come back
and take you to be
with me that you
also may be where
I am."*

John 14:3 NIV

NOTES

_____
_____
_____
_____
_____
_____
_____
_____
_____
_____
_____
_____
_____
_____
_____
_____
_____

JUN

To Do

- [ ] _____
- [ ] _____
- [ ] _____
- [ ] _____
- [ ] _____
- [ ] _____
- [ ] _____
- [ ] _____
- [ ] _____
- [ ] _____
- [ ] _____
- [ ] _____
- [ ] _____
- [ ] _____

JUNE

> *His divine power has granted to us everything pertaining to life and godliness, through the true knowledge of Him who called us by His own glory and excellence.*
>
> 2 Peter 1:3 NASB

MONDAY 18	TUESDAY 19	WEDNESDAY 20
07:00 AM	07:00 AM	07:00 AM
07:30 AM	07:30 AM	07:30 AM
08:00 AM	08:00 AM	08:00 AM
08:30 AM	08:30 AM	08:30 AM
09:00 AM	09:00 AM	09:00 AM
09:30 AM	09:30 AM	09:30 AM
10:00 AM	10:00 AM	10:00 AM
10:30 AM	10:30 AM	10:30 AM
11:00 AM	11:00 AM	11:00 AM
11:30 AM	11:30 AM	11:30 AM
12:00 PM	12:00 PM	12:00 PM
12:30 PM	12:30 PM	12:30 PM
01:00 PM	01:00 PM	01:00 PM
01:30 PM	01:30 PM	01:30 PM
02:00 PM	02:00 PM	02:00 PM
02:30 PM	02:30 PM	02:30 PM
03:00 PM	03:00 PM	03:00 PM
03:30 PM	03:30 PM	03:30 PM
04:00 PM	04:00 PM	04:00 PM
04:30 PM	04:30 PM	04:30 PM
05:00 PM	05:00 PM	05:00 PM
05:30 PM	05:30 PM	05:30 PM
06:00 PM	06:00 PM	06:00 PM
06:30 PM	06:30 PM	06:30 PM
07:00 PM	07:00 PM	07:00 PM
07:30 PM	07:30 PM	07:30 PM
08:00 PM	08:00 PM	08:00 PM
08:30 PM	08:30 PM	08:30 PM

MAY 2018

S	M	T	W	T	F	S
		1	2	3	4	5
6	7	8	9	10	11	12
13	14	15	16	17	18	19
20	21	22	23	24	25	26
27	28	29	30	31		

JUNE 2018

S	M	T	W	T	F	S
					1	2
3	4	5	6	7	8	9
10	11	12	13	14	15	16
17	18	19	20	21	22	23
24	25	26	27	28	29	30

JULY 2018

S	M	T	W	T	F	S
1	2	3	4	5	6	7
8	9	10	11	12	13	14
15	16	17	18	19	20	21
22	23	24	25	26	27	28
29	30	31				

JUNE

THURSDAY 21
Summer Solstice

07:00 AM
07:30 AM
08:00 AM
08:30 AM
09:00 AM
09:30 AM
10:00 AM
10:30 AM
11:00 AM
11:30 AM
12:00 PM
12:30 PM
01:00 PM
01:30 PM
02:00 PM
02:30 PM
03:00 PM
03:30 PM
04:00 PM
04:30 PM
05:00 PM
05:30 PM
06:00 PM
06:30 PM
07:00 PM
07:30 PM
08:00 PM
08:30 PM

FRIDAY 22

07:00 AM
07:30 AM
08:00 AM
08:30 AM
09:00 AM
09:30 AM
10:00 AM
10:30 AM
11:00 AM
11:30 AM
12:00 PM
12:30 PM
01:00 PM
01:30 PM
02:00 PM
02:30 PM
03:00 PM
03:30 PM
04:00 PM
04:30 PM
05:00 PM
05:30 PM
06:00 PM
06:30 PM
07:00 PM
07:30 PM
08:00 PM
08:30 PM

SATURDAY 23

SUNDAY 24

JUN

JUNE

MAY 2018
S	M	T	W	T	F	S
		1	2	3	4	5
6	7	8	9	10	11	12
13	14	15	16	17	18	19
20	21	22	23	24	25	26
27	28	29	30	31		

JUNE 2018
S	M	T	W	T	F	S
					1	2
3	4	5	6	7	8	9
10	11	12	13	14	15	16
17	18	19	20	21	22	23
24	25	26	27	28	29	30

JULY 2018
S	M	T	W	T	F	S
1	2	3	4	5	6	7
8	9	10	11	12	13	14
15	16	17	18	19	20	21
22	23	24	25	26	27	28
29	30	31				

JUN

Prayer Requests

REFLECTIONS

"If you have faith like a grain of mustard seed, you will say to this mountain, 'Move from here to there,' and it will move, and nothing will be impossible for you."

Matthew 17:20 ESV

NOTES

JUN

To Do

- [ ]
- [ ]
- [ ]
- [ ]
- [ ]
- [ ]
- [ ]
- [ ]
- [ ]
- [ ]
- [ ]
- [ ]
- [ ]
- [ ]

JUNE

MONDAY 25	TUESDAY 26	WEDNESDAY 27
07:00 AM	07:00 AM	07:00 AM
07:30 AM	07:30 AM	07:30 AM
08:00 AM	08:00 AM	08:00 AM
08:30 AM	08:30 AM	08:30 AM
09:00 AM	09:00 AM	09:00 AM
09:30 AM	09:30 AM	09:30 AM
10:00 AM	10:00 AM	10:00 AM
10:30 AM	10:30 AM	10:30 AM
11:00 AM	11:00 AM	11:00 AM
11:30 AM	11:30 AM	11:30 AM
12:00 PM	12:00 PM	12:00 PM
12:30 PM	12:30 PM	12:30 PM
01:00 PM	01:00 PM	01:00 PM
01:30 PM	01:30 PM	01:30 PM
02:00 PM	02:00 PM	02:00 PM
02:30 PM	02:30 PM	02:30 PM
03:00 PM	03:00 PM	03:00 PM
03:30 PM	03:30 PM	03:30 PM
04:00 PM	04:00 PM	04:00 PM
04:30 PM	04:30 PM	04:30 PM
05:00 PM	05:00 PM	05:00 PM
05:30 PM	05:30 PM	05:30 PM
06:00 PM	06:00 PM	06:00 PM
06:30 PM	06:30 PM	06:30 PM
07:00 PM	07:00 PM	07:00 PM
07:30 PM	07:30 PM	07:30 PM
08:00 PM	08:00 PM	08:00 PM
08:30 PM	08:30 PM	08:30 PM

MAY 2018						
S	M	T	W	T	F	S
		1	2	3	4	5
6	7	8	9	10	11	12
13	14	15	16	17	18	19
20	21	22	23	24	25	26
27	28	29	30	31		

JUNE 2018						
S	M	T	W	T	F	S
					1	2
3	4	5	6	7	8	9
10	11	12	13	14	15	16
17	18	19	20	21	22	23
24	25	26	27	28	29	30

JULY 2018						
S	M	T	W	T	F	S
1	2	3	4	5	6	7
8	9	10	11	12	13	14
15	16	17	18	19	20	21
22	23	24	25	26	27	28
29	30	31				

JUNE

JUN

THURSDAY 28

07:00 AM
07:30 AM
08:00 AM
08:30 AM
09:00 AM
09:30 AM
10:00 AM
10:30 AM
11:00 AM
11:30 AM
12:00 PM
12:30 PM
01:00 PM
01:30 PM
02:00 PM
02:30 PM
03:00 PM
03:30 PM
04:00 PM
04:30 PM
05:00 PM
05:30 PM
06:00 PM
06:30 PM
07:00 PM
07:30 PM
08:00 PM
08:30 PM

FRIDAY 29

07:00 AM
07:30 AM
08:00 AM
08:30 AM
09:00 AM
09:30 AM
10:00 AM
10:30 AM
11:00 AM
11:30 AM
12:00 PM
12:30 PM
01:00 PM
01:30 PM
02:00 PM
02:30 PM
03:00 PM
03:30 PM
04:00 PM
04:30 PM
05:00 PM
05:30 PM
06:00 PM
06:30 PM
07:00 PM
07:30 PM
08:00 PM
08:30 PM

SATURDAY 30

SUNDAY 1

JUNE

MAY 2018

S	M	T	W	T	F	S
		1	2	3	4	5
6	7	8	9	10	11	12
13	14	15	16	17	18	19
20	21	22	23	24	25	26
27	28	29	30	31		

JUNE 2018

S	M	T	W	T	F	S
					1	2
3	4	5	6	7	8	9
10	11	12	13	14	15	16
17	18	19	20	21	22	23
24	25	26	27	28	29	30

JULY 2018

S	M	T	W	T	F	S
1	2	3	4	5	6	7
8	9	10	11	12	13	14
15	16	17	18	19	20	21
22	23	24	25	26	27	28
29	30	31				

Prayer Requests

REFLECTIONS

Therefore, whether you eat or drink, or whatever you do, do all to the glory of God.

1 Corinthians 10:31 NKJV

NOTES

_____
_____
_____
_____
_____
_____
_____
_____
_____
_____
_____
_____
_____
_____
_____
_____
_____

To Do

- [ ] _____
- [ ] _____
- [ ] _____
- [ ] _____
- [ ] _____
- [ ] _____
- [ ] _____
- [ ] _____
- [ ] _____
- [ ] _____
- [ ] _____
- [ ] _____
- [ ] _____
- [ ] _____

JULY
2018

*For you created my inmost being;
you knit me together in my
mother's womb.
I praise you because I am fearfully
and wonderfully made;
your works are wonderful,
I know that full well.*

PSALM 139:13-14 NIV

MY GOALS FOR THE MONTH

MONTH AT A GLANCE

SUNDAY	1
MONDAY	2
TUESDAY	3
WEDNESDAY	4
THURSDAY	5
FRIDAY	6
SATURDAY	7
SUNDAY	8
MONDAY	9
TUESDAY	10
WEDNESDAY	11
THURSDAY	12
FRIDAY	13
SATURDAY	14
SUNDAY	15
MONDAY	16
TUESDAY	17
WEDNESDAY	18
THURSDAY	19
FRIDAY	20
SATURDAY	21
SUNDAY	22
MONDAY	23
TUESDAY	24
WEDNESDAY	25
THURSDAY	26
FRIDAY	27
SATURDAY	28
SUNDAY	29
MONDAY	30
TUESDAY	31

JULY

MONDAY 2	TUESDAY 3	WEDNESDAY 4 — Independence Day
07:00 AM	07:00 AM	07:00 AM
07:30 AM	07:30 AM	07:30 AM
08:00 AM	08:00 AM	08:00 AM
08:30 AM	08:30 AM	08:30 AM
09:00 AM	09:00 AM	09:00 AM
09:30 AM	09:30 AM	09:30 AM
10:00 AM	10:00 AM	10:00 AM
10:30 AM	10:30 AM	10:30 AM
11:00 AM	11:00 AM	11:00 AM
11:30 AM	11:30 AM	11:30 AM
12:00 PM	12:00 PM	12:00 PM
12:30 PM	12:30 PM	12:30 PM
01:00 PM	01:00 PM	01:00 PM
01:30 PM	01:30 PM	01:30 PM
02:00 PM	02:00 PM	02:00 PM
02:30 PM	02:30 PM	02:30 PM
03:00 PM	03:00 PM	03:00 PM
03:30 PM	03:30 PM	03:30 PM
04:00 PM	04:00 PM	04:00 PM
04:30 PM	04:30 PM	04:30 PM
05:00 PM	05:00 PM	05:00 PM
05:30 PM	05:30 PM	05:30 PM
06:00 PM	06:00 PM	06:00 PM
06:30 PM	06:30 PM	06:30 PM
07:00 PM	07:00 PM	07:00 PM
07:30 PM	07:30 PM	07:30 PM
08:00 PM	08:00 PM	08:00 PM
08:30 PM	08:30 PM	08:30 PM

JUNE 2018
S	M	T	W	T	F	S
					1	2
3	4	5	6	7	8	9
10	11	12	13	14	15	16
17	18	19	20	21	22	23
24	25	26	27	28	29	30

JULY 2018
S	M	T	W	T	F	S
1	2	3	4	5	6	7
8	9	10	11	12	13	14
15	16	17	18	19	20	21
22	23	24	25	26	27	28
29	30	31				

AUGUST 2018
S	M	T	W	T	F	S
			1	2	3	4
5	6	7	8	9	10	11
12	13	14	15	16	17	18
19	20	21	22	23	24	25
26	27	28	29	30	31	

JULY

THURSDAY 5

07:00 AM
07:30 AM
08:00 AM
08:30 AM
09:00 AM
09:30 AM
10:00 AM
10:30 AM
11:00 AM
11:30 AM
12:00 PM
12:30 PM
01:00 PM
01:30 PM
02:00 PM
02:30 PM
03:00 PM
03:30 PM
04:00 PM
04:30 PM
05:00 PM
05:30 PM
06:00 PM
06:30 PM
07:00 PM
07:30 PM
08:00 PM
08:30 PM

FRIDAY 6

07:00 AM
07:30 AM
08:00 AM
08:30 AM
09:00 AM
09:30 AM
10:00 AM
10:30 AM
11:00 AM
11:30 AM
12:00 PM
12:30 PM
01:00 PM
01:30 PM
02:00 PM
02:30 PM
03:00 PM
03:30 PM
04:00 PM
04:30 PM
05:00 PM
05:30 PM
06:00 PM
06:30 PM
07:00 PM
07:30 PM
08:00 PM
08:30 PM

SATURDAY 7

SUNDAY 8

JUL

JULY

JUNE 2018
S M T W T F S
            1 2
3 4 5 6 7 8 9
10 11 12 13 14 15 16
17 18 19 20 21 22 23
24 25 26 27 28 29 30

JULY 2018
S M T W T F S
1 2 3 4 5 6 7
8 9 10 11 12 13 14
15 16 17 18 19 20 21
22 23 24 25 26 27 28
29 30 31

AUGUST 2018
S M T W T F S
         1 2 3 4
5 6 7 8 9 10 11
12 13 14 15 16 17 18
19 20 21 22 23 24 25
26 27 28 29 30 31

Prayer Requests

_____
_____
_____
_____
_____
_____
_____
_____
_____
_____

JUL

REFLECTIONS

*Without faith
it is impossible
to please God,
because anyone
who comes to
him must believe
that he exists and
that he rewards
those who
earnestly
seek him.*

Hebrews 11:6 NIV

NOTES

To Do

JULY

MONDAY 9	TUESDAY 10	WEDNESDAY 11
07:00 AM	07:00 AM	07:00 AM
07:30 AM	07:30 AM	07:30 AM
08:00 AM	08:00 AM	08:00 AM
08:30 AM	08:30 AM	08:30 AM
09:00 AM	09:00 AM	09:00 AM
09:30 AM	09:30 AM	09:30 AM
10:00 AM	10:00 AM	10:00 AM
10:30 AM	10:30 AM	10:30 AM
11:00 AM	11:00 AM	11:00 AM
11:30 AM	11:30 AM	11:30 AM
12:00 PM	12:00 PM	12:00 PM
12:30 PM	12:30 PM	12:30 PM
01:00 PM	01:00 PM	01:00 PM
01:30 PM	01:30 PM	01:30 PM
02:00 PM	02:00 PM	02:00 PM
02:30 PM	02:30 PM	02:30 PM
03:00 PM	03:00 PM	03:00 PM
03:30 PM	03:30 PM	03:30 PM
04:00 PM	04:00 PM	04:00 PM
04:30 PM	04:30 PM	04:30 PM
05:00 PM	05:00 PM	05:00 PM
05:30 PM	05:30 PM	05:30 PM
06:00 PM	06:00 PM	06:00 PM
06:30 PM	06:30 PM	06:30 PM
07:00 PM	07:00 PM	07:00 PM
07:30 PM	07:30 PM	07:30 PM
08:00 PM	08:00 PM	08:00 PM
08:30 PM	08:30 PM	08:30 PM

JUNE 2018

S	M	T	W	T	F	S
					1	2
3	4	5	6	7	8	9
10	11	12	13	14	15	16
17	18	19	20	21	22	23
24	25	26	27	28	29	30

JULY 2018

S	M	T	W	T	F	S
1	2	3	4	5	6	7
8	9	10	11	12	13	14
15	16	17	18	19	20	21
22	23	24	25	26	27	28
29	30	31				

AUGUST 2018

S	M	T	W	T	F	S
			1	2	3	4
5	6	7	8	9	10	11
12	13	14	15	16	17	18
19	20	21	22	23	24	25
26	27	28	29	30	31	

JULY

THURSDAY 12

07:00 AM
07:30 AM
08:00 AM
08:30 AM
09:00 AM
09:30 AM
10:00 AM
10:30 AM
11:00 AM
11:30 AM
12:00 PM
12:30 PM
01:00 PM
01:30 PM
02:00 PM
02:30 PM
03:00 PM
03:30 PM
04:00 PM
04:30 PM
05:00 PM
05:30 PM
06:00 PM
06:30 PM
07:00 PM
07:30 PM
08:00 PM
08:30 PM

FRIDAY 13

07:00 AM
07:30 AM
08:00 AM
08:30 AM
09:00 AM
09:30 AM
10:00 AM
10:30 AM
11:00 AM
11:30 AM
12:00 PM
12:30 PM
01:00 PM
01:30 PM
02:00 PM
02:30 PM
03:00 PM
03:30 PM
04:00 PM
04:30 PM
05:00 PM
05:30 PM
06:00 PM
06:30 PM
07:00 PM
07:30 PM
08:00 PM
08:30 PM

SATURDAY 14

SUNDAY 15

JULY

JUNE 2018
S M T W T F S
                1 2
3 4 5 6 7 8 9
10 11 12 13 14 15 16
17 18 19 20 21 22 23
24 25 26 27 28 29 30

JULY 2018
S M T W T F S
1 2 3 4 5 6 7
8 9 10 11 12 13 14
15 16 17 18 19 20 21
22 23 24 25 26 27 28
29 30 31

AUGUST 2018
S M T W T F S
          1 2 3 4
5 6 7 8 9 10 11
12 13 14 15 16 17 18
19 20 21 22 23 24 25
26 27 28 29 30 31

Prayer Requests

_____
_____
_____
_____
_____
_____
_____
_____
_____
_____

JUL

REFLECTIONS

God is faithful.
He will not allow
the temptation
to be more than
you can stand.
When you are
tempted, he will
show you a way
out so that you
can endure.

1 Corinthians
10:13 NLT

NOTES

To Do

JULY

The name of the LORD is a strong tower;
The righteous runs into it and is safe.

Proverbs 18:10 NASB

JUL

MONDAY 16	TUESDAY 17	WEDNESDAY 18
07:00 AM	07:00 AM	07:00 AM
07:30 AM	07:30 AM	07:30 AM
08:00 AM	08:00 AM	08:00 AM
08:30 AM	08:30 AM	08:30 AM
09:00 AM	09:00 AM	09:00 AM
09:30 AM	09:30 AM	09:30 AM
10:00 AM	10:00 AM	10:00 AM
10:30 AM	10:30 AM	10:30 AM
11:00 AM	11:00 AM	11:00 AM
11:30 AM	11:30 AM	11:30 AM
12:00 PM	12:00 PM	12:00 PM
12:30 PM	12:30 PM	12:30 PM
01:00 PM	01:00 PM	01:00 PM
01:30 PM	01:30 PM	01:30 PM
02:00 PM	02:00 PM	02:00 PM
02:30 PM	02:30 PM	02:30 PM
03:00 PM	03:00 PM	03:00 PM
03:30 PM	03:30 PM	03:30 PM
04:00 PM	04:00 PM	04:00 PM
04:30 PM	04:30 PM	04:30 PM
05:00 PM	05:00 PM	05:00 PM
05:30 PM	05:30 PM	05:30 PM
06:00 PM	06:00 PM	06:00 PM
06:30 PM	06:30 PM	06:30 PM
07:00 PM	07:00 PM	07:00 PM
07:30 PM	07:30 PM	07:30 PM
08:00 PM	08:00 PM	08:00 PM
08:30 PM	08:30 PM	08:30 PM

JUNE 2018

S	M	T	W	T	F	S
					1	2
3	4	5	6	7	8	9
10	11	12	13	14	15	16
17	18	19	20	21	22	23
24	25	26	27	28	29	30

JULY 2018

S	M	T	W	T	F	S
1	2	3	4	5	6	7
8	9	10	11	12	13	14
15	16	17	18	19	20	21
22	23	24	25	26	27	28
29	30	31				

AUGUST 2018

S	M	T	W	T	F	S
			1	2	3	4
5	6	7	8	9	10	11
12	13	14	15	16	17	18
19	20	21	22	23	24	25
26	27	28	29	30	31	

THURSDAY 19

- 07:00 AM
- 07:30 AM
- 08:00 AM
- 08:30 AM
- 09:00 AM
- 09:30 AM
- 10:00 AM
- 10:30 AM
- 11:00 AM
- 11:30 AM
- 12:00 PM
- 12:30 PM
- 01:00 PM
- 01:30 PM
- 02:00 PM
- 02:30 PM
- 03:00 PM
- 03:30 PM
- 04:00 PM
- 04:30 PM
- 05:00 PM
- 05:30 PM
- 06:00 PM
- 06:30 PM
- 07:00 PM
- 07:30 PM
- 08:00 PM
- 08:30 PM

FRIDAY 20

- 07:00 AM
- 07:30 AM
- 08:00 AM
- 08:30 AM
- 09:00 AM
- 09:30 AM
- 10:00 AM
- 10:30 AM
- 11:00 AM
- 11:30 AM
- 12:00 PM
- 12:30 PM
- 01:00 PM
- 01:30 PM
- 02:00 PM
- 02:30 PM
- 03:00 PM
- 03:30 PM
- 04:00 PM
- 04:30 PM
- 05:00 PM
- 05:30 PM
- 06:00 PM
- 06:30 PM
- 07:00 PM
- 07:30 PM
- 08:00 PM
- 08:30 PM

SATURDAY 21

SUNDAY 22

JULY

JUNE 2018
S	M	T	W	T	F	S
					1	2
3	4	5	6	7	8	9
10	11	12	13	14	15	16
17	18	19	20	21	22	23
24	25	26	27	28	29	30

JULY 2018
S	M	T	W	T	F	S
1	2	3	4	5	6	7
8	9	10	11	12	13	14
15	16	17	18	19	20	21
22	23	24	25	26	27	28
29	30	31				

AUGUST 2018
S	M	T	W	T	F	S
			1	2	3	4
5	6	7	8	9	10	11
12	13	14	15	16	17	18
19	20	21	22	23	24	25
26	27	28	29	30	31	

Prayer Requests

JUL

REFLECTIONS

When you lie down, you will not be afraid; when you lie down, your sleep will be sweet.

Proverbs 3:24 NIV

NOTES

To Do

JULY

MONDAY 23	TUESDAY 24	WEDNESDAY 25
07:00 AM	07:00 AM	07:00 AM
07:30 AM	07:30 AM	07:30 AM
08:00 AM	08:00 AM	08:00 AM
08:30 AM	08:30 AM	08:30 AM
09:00 AM	09:00 AM	09:00 AM
09:30 AM	09:30 AM	09:30 AM
10:00 AM	10:00 AM	10:00 AM
10:30 AM	10:30 AM	10:30 AM
11:00 AM	11:00 AM	11:00 AM
11:30 AM	11:30 AM	11:30 AM
12:00 PM	12:00 PM	12:00 PM
12:30 PM	12:30 PM	12:30 PM
01:00 PM	01:00 PM	01:00 PM
01:30 PM	01:30 PM	01:30 PM
02:00 PM	02:00 PM	02:00 PM
02:30 PM	02:30 PM	02:30 PM
03:00 PM	03:00 PM	03:00 PM
03:30 PM	03:30 PM	03:30 PM
04:00 PM	04:00 PM	04:00 PM
04:30 PM	04:30 PM	04:30 PM
05:00 PM	05:00 PM	05:00 PM
05:30 PM	05:30 PM	05:30 PM
06:00 PM	06:00 PM	06:00 PM
06:30 PM	06:30 PM	06:30 PM
07:00 PM	07:00 PM	07:00 PM
07:30 PM	07:30 PM	07:30 PM
08:00 PM	08:00 PM	08:00 PM
08:30 PM	08:30 PM	08:30 PM

JUL

JUNE 2018
S	M	T	W	T	F	S
					1	2
3	4	5	6	7	8	9
10	11	12	13	14	15	16
17	18	19	20	21	22	23
24	25	26	27	28	29	30

JULY 2018
S	M	T	W	T	F	S
1	2	3	4	5	6	7
8	9	10	11	12	13	14
15	16	17	18	19	20	21
22	23	24	25	26	27	28
29	30	31				

AUGUST 2018
S	M	T	W	T	F	S
			1	2	3	4
5	6	7	8	9	10	11
12	13	14	15	16	17	18
19	20	21	22	23	24	25
26	27	28	29	30	31	

JULY

JUL

THURSDAY 26

07:00 AM
07:30 AM
08:00 AM
08:30 AM
09:00 AM
09:30 AM
10:00 AM
10:30 AM
11:00 AM
11:30 AM
12:00 PM
12:30 PM
01:00 PM
01:30 PM
02:00 PM
02:30 PM
03:00 PM
03:30 PM
04:00 PM
04:30 PM
05:00 PM
05:30 PM
06:00 PM
06:30 PM
07:00 PM
07:30 PM
08:00 PM
08:30 PM

FRIDAY 27

07:00 AM
07:30 AM
08:00 AM
08:30 AM
09:00 AM
09:30 AM
10:00 AM
10:30 AM
11:00 AM
11:30 AM
12:00 PM
12:30 PM
01:00 PM
01:30 PM
02:00 PM
02:30 PM
03:00 PM
03:30 PM
04:00 PM
04:30 PM
05:00 PM
05:30 PM
06:00 PM
06:30 PM
07:00 PM
07:30 PM
08:00 PM
08:30 PM

SATURDAY 28

SUNDAY 29

JULY

JUNE 2018
S	M	T	W	T	F	S
					1	2
3	4	5	6	7	8	9
10	11	12	13	14	15	16
17	18	19	20	21	22	23
24	25	26	27	28	29	30

JULY 2018
S	M	T	W	T	F	S
1	2	3	4	5	6	7
8	9	10	11	12	13	14
15	16	17	18	19	20	21
22	23	24	25	26	27	28
29	30	31				

AUGUST 2018
S	M	T	W	T	F	S
			1	2	3	4
5	6	7	8	9	10	11
12	13	14	15	16	17	18
19	20	21	22	23	24	25
26	27	28	29	30	31	

Prayer Requests

JUL

REFLECTIONS

For God has not given us a spirit of fear, but of power and of love and of a sound mind.

2 Timothy 1:7 NKJV

NOTES

To Do

AUGUST

2018

Consider it pure joy, my brothers and sisters, whenever you face trials of many kinds, because you know that the testing of your faith produces perseverance.

JAMES 1:2-3 NIV

MY GOALS FOR THE MONTH

_____
_____
_____
_____
_____
_____
_____
_____
_____
_____
_____
_____
_____
_____
_____
_____
_____

MONTH AT A GLANCE

WEDNESDAY	1	
THURSDAY	2	
FRIDAY	3	
SATURDAY	4	
SUNDAY	5	
MONDAY	6	
TUESDAY	7	
WEDNESDAY	8	
THURSDAY	9	
FRIDAY	10	
SATURDAY	11	
SUNDAY	12	
MONDAY	13	
TUESDAY	14	
WEDNESDAY	15	
THURSDAY	16	
FRIDAY	17	
SATURDAY	18	
SUNDAY	19	
MONDAY	20	
TUESDAY	21	
WEDNESDAY	22	
THURSDAY	23	
FRIDAY	24	
SATURDAY	25	
SUNDAY	26	
MONDAY	27	
TUESDAY	28	
WEDNESDAY	29	
THURSDAY	30	
FRIDAY	31	

AUGUST

MONDAY 30	TUESDAY 31	WEDNESDAY 1
07:00 AM	07:00 AM	07:00 AM
07:30 AM	07:30 AM	07:30 AM
08:00 AM	08:00 AM	08:00 AM
08:30 AM	08:30 AM	08:30 AM
09:00 AM	09:00 AM	09:00 AM
09:30 AM	09:30 AM	09:30 AM
10:00 AM	10:00 AM	10:00 AM
10:30 AM	10:30 AM	10:30 AM
11:00 AM	11:00 AM	11:00 AM
11:30 AM	11:30 AM	11:30 AM
12:00 PM	12:00 PM	12:00 PM
12:30 PM	12:30 PM	12:30 PM
01:00 PM	01:00 PM	01:00 PM
01:30 PM	01:30 PM	01:30 PM
02:00 PM	02:00 PM	02:00 PM
02:30 PM	02:30 PM	02:30 PM
03:00 PM	03:00 PM	03:00 PM
03:30 PM	03:30 PM	03:30 PM
04:00 PM	04:00 PM	04:00 PM
04:30 PM	04:30 PM	04:30 PM
05:00 PM	05:00 PM	05:00 PM
05:30 PM	05:30 PM	05:30 PM
06:00 PM	06:00 PM	06:00 PM
06:30 PM	06:30 PM	06:30 PM
07:00 PM	07:00 PM	07:00 PM
07:30 PM	07:30 PM	07:30 PM
08:00 PM	08:00 PM	08:00 PM
08:30 PM	08:30 PM	08:30 PM

AUG

JULY 2018						
S	M	T	W	T	F	S
1	2	3	4	5	6	7
8	9	10	11	12	13	14
15	16	17	18	19	20	21
22	23	24	25	26	27	28
29	30	31				

AUGUST 2018						
S	M	T	W	T	F	S
			1	2	3	4
5	6	7	8	9	10	11
12	13	14	15	16	17	18
19	20	21	22	23	24	25
26	27	28	29	30	31	

SEPTEMBER 2018						
S	M	T	W	T	F	S
						1
2	3	4	5	6	7	8
9	10	11	12	13	14	15
16	17	18	19	20	21	22
23	24	25	26	27	28	29
30						

AUGUST

THURSDAY 2

07:00 AM
07:30 AM
08:00 AM
08:30 AM
09:00 AM
09:30 AM
10:00 AM
10:30 AM
11:00 AM
11:30 AM
12:00 PM
12:30 PM
01:00 PM
01:30 PM
02:00 PM
02:30 PM
03:00 PM
03:30 PM
04:00 PM
04:30 PM
05:00 PM
05:30 PM
06:00 PM
06:30 PM
07:00 PM
07:30 PM
08:00 PM
08:30 PM

FRIDAY 3

07:00 AM
07:30 AM
08:00 AM
08:30 AM
09:00 AM
09:30 AM
10:00 AM
10:30 AM
11:00 AM
11:30 AM
12:00 PM
12:30 PM
01:00 PM
01:30 PM
02:00 PM
02:30 PM
03:00 PM
03:30 PM
04:00 PM
04:30 PM
05:00 PM
05:30 PM
06:00 PM
06:30 PM
07:00 PM
07:30 PM
08:00 PM
08:30 PM

SATURDAY 4

SUNDAY 5

AUG

AUGUST

JULY 2018

S	M	T	W	T	F	S
1	2	3	4	5	6	7
8	9	10	11	12	13	14
15	16	17	18	19	20	21
22	23	24	25	26	27	28
29	30	31				

AUGUST 2018

S	M	T	W	T	F	S
			1	2	3	4
5	6	7	8	9	10	11
12	13	14	15	16	17	18
19	20	21	22	23	24	25
26	27	28	29	30	31	

SEPTEMBER 2018

S	M	T	W	T	F	S
						1
2	3	4	5	6	7	8
9	10	11	12	13	14	15
16	17	18	19	20	21	22
23	24	25	26	27	28	29
30						

Prayer Requests

REFLECTIONS

O Lord,
You are our Father;
We are the clay,
and You our potter;
And all we are the
work of Your hand.

Isaiah 64:8 NKJV

AUG

NOTES

To Do

- [ ]
- [ ]
- [ ]
- [ ]
- [ ]
- [ ]
- [ ]
- [ ]
- [ ]
- [ ]
- [ ]
- [ ]
- [ ]
- [ ]
- [ ]

AUGUST

MONDAY
6

07:00 AM
07:30 AM
08:00 AM
08:30 AM
09:00 AM
09:30 AM
10:00 AM
10:30 AM
11:00 AM
11:30 AM
12:00 PM
12:30 PM
01:00 PM
01:30 PM
02:00 PM
02:30 PM
03:00 PM
03:30 PM
04:00 PM
04:30 PM
05:00 PM
05:30 PM
06:00 PM
06:30 PM
07:00 PM
07:30 PM
08:00 PM
08:30 PM

TUESDAY
7

07:00 AM
07:30 AM
08:00 AM
08:30 AM
09:00 AM
09:30 AM
10:00 AM
10:30 AM
11:00 AM
11:30 AM
12:00 PM
12:30 PM
01:00 PM
01:30 PM
02:00 PM
02:30 PM
03:00 PM
03:30 PM
04:00 PM
04:30 PM
05:00 PM
05:30 PM
06:00 PM
06:30 PM
07:00 PM
07:30 PM
08:00 PM
08:30 PM

WEDNESDAY
8

07:00 AM
07:30 AM
08:00 AM
08:30 AM
09:00 AM
09:30 AM
10:00 AM
10:30 AM
11:00 AM
11:30 AM
12:00 PM
12:30 PM
01:00 PM
01:30 PM
02:00 PM
02:30 PM
03:00 PM
03:30 PM
04:00 PM
04:30 PM
05:00 PM
05:30 PM
06:00 PM
06:30 PM
07:00 PM
07:30 PM
08:00 PM
08:30 PM

A
U
G

JULY 2018

S	M	T	W	T	F	S
1	2	3	4	5	6	7
8	9	10	11	12	13	14
15	16	17	18	19	20	21
22	23	24	25	26	27	28
29	30	31				

AUGUST 2018

S	M	T	W	T	F	S
			1	2	3	4
5	6	7	8	9	10	11
12	13	14	15	16	17	18
19	20	21	22	23	24	25
26	27	28	29	30	31	

SEPTEMBER 2018

S	M	T	W	T	F	S
						1
2	3	4	5	6	7	8
9	10	11	12	13	14	15
16	17	18	19	20	21	22
23	24	25	26	27	28	29
30						

AUGUST

THURSDAY 9

07:00 AM
07:30 AM
08:00 AM
08:30 AM
09:00 AM
09:30 AM
10:00 AM
10:30 AM
11:00 AM
11:30 AM
12:00 PM
12:30 PM
01:00 PM
01:30 PM
02:00 PM
02:30 PM
03:00 PM
03:30 PM
04:00 PM
04:30 PM
05:00 PM
05:30 PM
06:00 PM
06:30 PM
07:00 PM
07:30 PM
08:00 PM
08:30 PM

FRIDAY 10

07:00 AM
07:30 AM
08:00 AM
08:30 AM
09:00 AM
09:30 AM
10:00 AM
10:30 AM
11:00 AM
11:30 AM
12:00 PM
12:30 PM
01:00 PM
01:30 PM
02:00 PM
02:30 PM
03:00 PM
03:30 PM
04:00 PM
04:30 PM
05:00 PM
05:30 PM
06:00 PM
06:30 PM
07:00 PM
07:30 PM
08:00 PM
08:30 PM

SATURDAY 11

SUNDAY 12

A
U
G

AUGUST

JULY 2018
S	M	T	W	T	F	S
1	2	3	4	5	6	7
8	9	10	11	12	13	14
15	16	17	18	19	20	21
22	23	24	25	26	27	28
29	30	31				

AUGUST 2018
S	M	T	W	T	F	S
			1	2	3	4
5	6	7	8	9	10	11
12	13	14	15	16	17	18
19	20	21	22	23	24	25
26	27	28	29	30	31	

SEPTEMBER 2018
S	M	T	W	T	F	S
						1
2	3	4	5	6	7	8
9	10	11	12	13	14	15
16	17	18	19	20	21	22
23	24	25	26	27	28	29
30						

Prayer Requests

REFLECTIONS

AUG

He is so rich in kindness and grace that he purchased our freedom with the blood of his Son and forgave our sins.

Ephesians 1:7 NLT

NOTES

To Do

- [ ]
- [ ]
- [ ]
- [ ]
- [ ]
- [ ]
- [ ]
- [ ]
- [ ]
- [ ]
- [ ]
- [ ]
- [ ]
- [ ]
- [ ]

AUGUST

MONDAY 13	TUESDAY 14	WEDNESDAY 15
07:00 AM	07:00 AM	07:00 AM
07:30 AM	07:30 AM	07:30 AM
08:00 AM	08:00 AM	08:00 AM
08:30 AM	08:30 AM	08:30 AM
09:00 AM	09:00 AM	09:00 AM
09:30 AM	09:30 AM	09:30 AM
10:00 AM	10:00 AM	10:00 AM
10:30 AM	10:30 AM	10:30 AM
11:00 AM	11:00 AM	11:00 AM
11:30 AM	11:30 AM	11:30 AM
12:00 PM	12:00 PM	12:00 PM
12:30 PM	12:30 PM	12:30 PM
01:00 PM	01:00 PM	01:00 PM
01:30 PM	01:30 PM	01:30 PM
02:00 PM	02:00 PM	02:00 PM
02:30 PM	02:30 PM	02:30 PM
03:00 PM	03:00 PM	03:00 PM
03:30 PM	03:30 PM	03:30 PM
04:00 PM	04:00 PM	04:00 PM
04:30 PM	04:30 PM	04:30 PM
05:00 PM	05:00 PM	05:00 PM
05:30 PM	05:30 PM	05:30 PM
06:00 PM	06:00 PM	06:00 PM
06:30 PM	06:30 PM	06:30 PM
07:00 PM	07:00 PM	07:00 PM
07:30 PM	07:30 PM	07:30 PM
08:00 PM	08:00 PM	08:00 PM
08:30 PM	08:30 PM	08:30 PM

AUG

JULY 2018

S	M	T	W	T	F	S
1	2	3	4	5	6	7
8	9	10	11	12	13	14
15	16	17	18	19	20	21
22	23	24	25	26	27	28
29	30	31				

AUGUST 2018

S	M	T	W	T	F	S
			1	2	3	4
5	6	7	8	9	10	11
12	13	14	15	16	17	18
19	20	21	22	23	24	25
26	27	28	29	30	31	

SEPTEMBER 2018

S	M	T	W	T	F	S
						1
2	3	4	5	6	7	8
9	10	11	12	13	14	15
16	17	18	19	20	21	22
23	24	25	26	27	28	29
30						

AUGUST

THURSDAY 16

07:00 AM
07:30 AM
08:00 AM
08:30 AM
09:00 AM
09:30 AM
10:00 AM
10:30 AM
11:00 AM
11:30 AM
12:00 PM
12:30 PM
01:00 PM
01:30 PM
02:00 PM
02:30 PM
03:00 PM
03:30 PM
04:00 PM
04:30 PM
05:00 PM
05:30 PM
06:00 PM
06:30 PM
07:00 PM
07:30 PM
08:00 PM
08:30 PM

FRIDAY 17

07:00 AM
07:30 AM
08:00 AM
08:30 AM
09:00 AM
09:30 AM
10:00 AM
10:30 AM
11:00 AM
11:30 AM
12:00 PM
12:30 PM
01:00 PM
01:30 PM
02:00 PM
02:30 PM
03:00 PM
03:30 PM
04:00 PM
04:30 PM
05:00 PM
05:30 PM
06:00 PM
06:30 PM
07:00 PM
07:30 PM
08:00 PM
08:30 PM

SATURDAY 18

SUNDAY 19

A
U
G

AUGUST

JULY 2018
S	M	T	W	T	F	S
1	2	3	4	5	6	7
8	9	10	11	12	13	14
15	16	17	18	19	20	21
22	23	24	25	26	27	28
29	30	31				

AUGUST 2018
S	M	T	W	T	F	S
			1	2	3	4
5	6	7	8	9	10	11
12	13	14	15	16	17	18
19	20	21	22	23	24	25
26	27	28	29	30	31	

SEPTEMBER 2018
S	M	T	W	T	F	S
						1
2	3	4	5	6	7	8
9	10	11	12	13	14	15
16	17	18	19	20	21	22
23	24	25	26	27	28	29
30						

Prayer Requests

AUG

REFLECTIONS

*Lord, are good,
and ready to
forgive,
And abundant
in mercy to all
those who call
upon You.*

Psalm 86:5 NKJV

NOTES

To Do

AUGUST

AUG

MONDAY 20	TUESDAY 21	WEDNESDAY 22
07:00 AM	07:00 AM	07:00 AM
07:30 AM	07:30 AM	07:30 AM
08:00 AM	08:00 AM	08:00 AM
08:30 AM	08:30 AM	08:30 AM
09:00 AM	09:00 AM	09:00 AM
09:30 AM	09:30 AM	09:30 AM
10:00 AM	10:00 AM	10:00 AM
10:30 AM	10:30 AM	10:30 AM
11:00 AM	11:00 AM	11:00 AM
11:30 AM	11:30 AM	11:30 AM
12:00 PM	12:00 PM	12:00 PM
12:30 PM	12:30 PM	12:30 PM
01:00 PM	01:00 PM	01:00 PM
01:30 PM	01:30 PM	01:30 PM
02:00 PM	02:00 PM	02:00 PM
02:30 PM	02:30 PM	02:30 PM
03:00 PM	03:00 PM	03:00 PM
03:30 PM	03:30 PM	03:30 PM
04:00 PM	04:00 PM	04:00 PM
04:30 PM	04:30 PM	04:30 PM
05:00 PM	05:00 PM	05:00 PM
05:30 PM	05:30 PM	05:30 PM
06:00 PM	06:00 PM	06:00 PM
06:30 PM	06:30 PM	06:30 PM
07:00 PM	07:00 PM	07:00 PM
07:30 PM	07:30 PM	07:30 PM
08:00 PM	08:00 PM	08:00 PM
08:30 PM	08:30 PM	08:30 PM

JULY 2018
S	M	T	W	T	F	S
1	2	3	4	5	6	7
8	9	10	11	12	13	14
15	16	17	18	19	20	21
22	23	24	25	26	27	28
29	30	31				

AUGUST 2018
S	M	T	W	T	F	S
			1	2	3	4
5	6	7	8	9	10	11
12	13	14	15	16	17	18
19	20	21	22	23	24	25
26	27	28	29	30	31	

SEPTEMBER 2018
S	M	T	W	T	F	S
						1
2	3	4	5	6	7	8
9	10	11	12	13	14	15
16	17	18	19	20	21	22
23	24	25	26	27	28	29
30						

AUGUST

THURSDAY 23

07:00 AM
07:30 AM
08:00 AM
08:30 AM
09:00 AM
09:30 AM
10:00 AM
10:30 AM
11:00 AM
11:30 AM
12:00 PM
12:30 PM
01:00 PM
01:30 PM
02:00 PM
02:30 PM
03:00 PM
03:30 PM
04:00 PM
04:30 PM
05:00 PM
05:30 PM
06:00 PM
06:30 PM
07:00 PM
07:30 PM
08:00 PM
08:30 PM

FRIDAY 24

07:00 AM
07:30 AM
08:00 AM
08:30 AM
09:00 AM
09:30 AM
10:00 AM
10:30 AM
11:00 AM
11:30 AM
12:00 PM
12:30 PM
01:00 PM
01:30 PM
02:00 PM
02:30 PM
03:00 PM
03:30 PM
04:00 PM
04:30 PM
05:00 PM
05:30 PM
06:00 PM
06:30 PM
07:00 PM
07:30 PM
08:00 PM
08:30 PM

SATURDAY 25

SUNDAY 26

AUGUST

JULY 2018
S	M	T	W	T	F	S
1	2	3	4	5	6	7
8	9	10	11	12	13	14
15	16	17	18	19	20	21
22	23	24	25	26	27	28
29	30	31				

AUGUST 2018
S	M	T	W	T	F	S
			1	2	3	4
5	6	7	8	9	10	11
12	13	14	15	16	17	18
19	20	21	22	23	24	25
26	27	28	29	30	31	

SEPTEMBER 2018
S	M	T	W	T	F	S
						1
2	3	4	5	6	7	8
9	10	11	12	13	14	15
16	17	18	19	20	21	22
23	24	25	26	27	28	29
30						

Prayer Requests

AUG

REFLECTIONS

Whoever is generous to the poor lends to the Lord, and he will repay him for his deed.

Proverbs 19:17
ESV

NOTES

To Do

AUG

AUGUST

"Take my yoke upon you, and learn from me, for I am gentle and lowly in heart, and you will find rest your souls."

Matthew 11:29-30 ESV

AUG

MONDAY 27	TUESDAY 28	WEDNESDAY 29
07:00 AM	07:00 AM	07:00 AM
07:30 AM	07:30 AM	07:30 AM
08:00 AM	08:00 AM	08:00 AM
08:30 AM	08:30 AM	08:30 AM
09:00 AM	09:00 AM	09:00 AM
09:30 AM	09:30 AM	09:30 AM
10:00 AM	10:00 AM	10:00 AM
10:30 AM	10:30 AM	10:30 AM
11:00 AM	11:00 AM	11:00 AM
11:30 AM	11:30 AM	11:30 AM
12:00 PM	12:00 PM	12:00 PM
12:30 PM	12:30 PM	12:30 PM
01:00 PM	01:00 PM	01:00 PM
01:30 PM	01:30 PM	01:30 PM
02:00 PM	02:00 PM	02:00 PM
02:30 PM	02:30 PM	02:30 PM
03:00 PM	03:00 PM	03:00 PM
03:30 PM	03:30 PM	03:30 PM
04:00 PM	04:00 PM	04:00 PM
04:30 PM	04:30 PM	04:30 PM
05:00 PM	05:00 PM	05:00 PM
05:30 PM	05:30 PM	05:30 PM
06:00 PM	06:00 PM	06:00 PM
06:30 PM	06:30 PM	06:30 PM
07:00 PM	07:00 PM	07:00 PM
07:30 PM	07:30 PM	07:30 PM
08:00 PM	08:00 PM	08:00 PM
08:30 PM	08:30 PM	08:30 PM

JULY 2018						
S	M	T	W	T	F	S
1	2	3	4	5	6	7
8	9	10	11	12	13	14
15	16	17	18	19	20	21
22	23	24	25	26	27	28
29	30	31				

AUGUST 2018						
S	M	T	W	T	F	S
			1	2	3	4
5	6	7	8	9	10	11
12	13	14	15	16	17	18
19	20	21	22	23	24	25
26	27	28	29	30	31	

SEPTEMBER 2018						
S	M	T	W	T	F	S
						1
2	3	4	5	6	7	8
9	10	11	12	13	14	15
16	17	18	19	20	21	22
23	24	25	26	27	28	29
30						

SEPTEMBER

THURSDAY 30

07:00 AM
07:30 AM
08:00 AM
08:30 AM
09:00 AM
09:30 AM
10:00 AM
10:30 AM
11:00 AM
11:30 AM
12:00 PM
12:30 PM
01:00 PM
01:30 PM
02:00 PM
02:30 PM
03:00 PM
03:30 PM
04:00 PM
04:30 PM
05:00 PM
05:30 PM
06:00 PM
06:30 PM
07:00 PM
07:30 PM
08:00 PM
08:30 PM

FRIDAY 31

07:00 AM
07:30 AM
08:00 AM
08:30 AM
09:00 AM
09:30 AM
10:00 AM
10:30 AM
11:00 AM
11:30 AM
12:00 PM
12:30 PM
01:00 PM
01:30 PM
02:00 PM
02:30 PM
03:00 PM
03:30 PM
04:00 PM
04:30 PM
05:00 PM
05:30 PM
06:00 PM
06:30 PM
07:00 PM
07:30 PM
08:00 PM
08:30 PM

SATURDAY 1

SUNDAY 2

AUGUST

JULY 2018

S	M	T	W	T	F	S
1	2	3	4	5	6	7
8	9	10	11	12	13	14
15	16	17	18	19	20	21
22	23	24	25	26	27	28
29	30	31				

AUGUST 2018

S	M	T	W	T	F	S
			1	2	3	4
5	6	7	8	9	10	11
12	13	14	15	16	17	18
19	20	21	22	23	24	25
26	27	28	29	30	31	

SEPTEMBER 2018

S	M	T	W	T	F	S
						1
2	3	4	5	6	7	8
9	10	11	12	13	14	15
16	17	18	19	20	21	22
23	24	25	26	27	28	29
30						

Prayer Requests

REFLECTIONS

"Blessed are the gentle, for they shall inherit the earth."

Matthew 5:5 NASB

AUG

NOTES

_____
_____
_____
_____
_____
_____
_____
_____
_____
_____
_____
_____
_____
_____
_____
_____
_____

To Do

- [ ] _____
- [ ] _____
- [ ] _____
- [ ] _____
- [ ] _____
- [ ] _____
- [ ] _____
- [ ] _____
- [ ] _____
- [ ] _____
- [ ] _____
- [ ] _____
- [ ] _____
- [ ] _____

SEPTEMBER

2018

We do not lose heart, but though our outer man is decaying, yet our inner man is being renewed day by day. For momentary, light affliction is producing for us an eternal weight of glory far beyond all comparison.

2 CORINTHIANS 4:16-17 NASB

MY GOALS FOR THE MONTH

MONTH AT A GLANCE

SATURDAY	1	
SUNDAY	2	
MONDAY	3	
TUESDAY	4	
WEDNESDAY	5	
THURSDAY	6	
FRIDAY	7	
SATURDAY	8	
SUNDAY	9	
MONDAY	10	
TUESDAY	11	
WEDNESDAY	12	
THURSDAY	13	
FRIDAY	14	
SATURDAY	15	
SUNDAY	16	
MONDAY	17	
TUESDAY	18	
WEDNESDAY	19	
THURSDAY	20	
FRIDAY	21	
SATURDAY	22	
SUNDAY	23	
MONDAY	24	
TUESDAY	25	
WEDNESDAY	26	
THURSDAY	27	
FRIDAY	28	
SATURDAY	29	
SUNDAY	30	

SEPTEMBER

SEPT

MONDAY 3 — Labor Day

07:00 AM
07:30 AM
08:00 AM
08:30 AM
09:00 AM
09:30 AM
10:00 AM
10:30 AM
11:00 AM
11:30 AM
12:00 PM
12:30 PM
01:00 PM
01:30 PM
02:00 PM
02:30 PM
03:00 PM
03:30 PM
04:00 PM
04:30 PM
05:00 PM
05:30 PM
06:00 PM
06:30 PM
07:00 PM
07:30 PM
08:00 PM
08:30 PM

TUESDAY 4

07:00 AM
07:30 AM
08:00 AM
08:30 AM
09:00 AM
09:30 AM
10:00 AM
10:30 AM
11:00 AM
11:30 AM
12:00 PM
12:30 PM
01:00 PM
01:30 PM
02:00 PM
02:30 PM
03:00 PM
03:30 PM
04:00 PM
04:30 PM
05:00 PM
05:30 PM
06:00 PM
06:30 PM
07:00 PM
07:30 PM
08:00 PM
08:30 PM

WEDNESDAY 5

07:00 AM
07:30 AM
08:00 AM
08:30 AM
09:00 AM
09:30 AM
10:00 AM
10:30 AM
11:00 AM
11:30 AM
12:00 PM
12:30 PM
01:00 PM
01:30 PM
02:00 PM
02:30 PM
03:00 PM
03:30 PM
04:00 PM
04:30 PM
05:00 PM
05:30 PM
06:00 PM
06:30 PM
07:00 PM
07:30 PM
08:00 PM
08:30 PM

AUGUST 2018
S M T W T F S
1 2 3 4
5 6 7 8 9 10 11
12 13 14 15 16 17 18
19 20 21 22 23 24 25
26 27 28 29 30 31

SEPTEMBER 2018
S M T W T F S
1
2 3 4 5 6 7 8
9 10 11 12 13 14 15
16 17 18 19 20 21 22
23 24 25 26 27 28 29
30

OCTOBER 2018
S M T W T F S
1 2 3 4 5 6
7 8 9 10 11 12 13
14 15 16 17 18 19 20
21 22 23 24 25 26 27
28 29 30 31

SEPTEMBER

THURSDAY 6

07:00 AM
07:30 AM
08:00 AM
08:30 AM
09:00 AM
09:30 AM
10:00 AM
10:30 AM
11:00 AM
11:30 AM
12:00 PM
12:30 PM
01:00 PM
01:30 PM
02:00 PM
02:30 PM
03:00 PM
03:30 PM
04:00 PM
04:30 PM
05:00 PM
05:30 PM
06:00 PM
06:30 PM
07:00 PM
07:30 PM
08:00 PM
08:30 PM

FRIDAY 7

07:00 AM
07:30 AM
08:00 AM
08:30 AM
09:00 AM
09:30 AM
10:00 AM
10:30 AM
11:00 AM
11:30 AM
12:00 PM
12:30 PM
01:00 PM
01:30 PM
02:00 PM
02:30 PM
03:00 PM
03:30 PM
04:00 PM
04:30 PM
05:00 PM
05:30 PM
06:00 PM
06:30 PM
07:00 PM
07:30 PM
08:00 PM
08:30 PM

SATURDAY 8

SUNDAY 9

Rosh Hashanah Begins

SEPT

SEPTEMBER

AUGUST 2018
S	M	T	W	T	F	S
			1	2	3	4
5	6	7	8	9	10	11
12	13	14	15	16	17	18
19	20	21	22	23	24	25
26	27	28	29	30	31	

SEPTEMBER 2018
S	M	T	W	T	F	S
						1
2	3	4	5	6	7	8
9	10	11	12	13	14	15
16	17	18	19	20	21	22
23	24	25	26	27	28	29
30						

OCTOBER 2018
S	M	T	W	T	F	S
	1	2	3	4	5	6
7	8	9	10	11	12	13
14	15	16	17	18	19	20
21	22	23	24	25	26	27
28	29	30	31			

Prayer Requests

REFLECTIONS

*The Lord is good
to all, and his
mercy is over all
that he has made.*

Psalm 145:9 ESV

SEPT

NOTES

To Do

- [ ]
- [ ]
- [ ]
- [ ]
- [ ]
- [ ]
- [ ]
- [ ]
- [ ]
- [ ]
- [ ]
- [ ]
- [ ]
- [ ]
- [ ]

SEPTEMBER

He will once again fill your mouth with laughter and your lips with shouts of joy.

Job 8:21 NLT

MONDAY
10

07:00 AM	
07:30 AM	
08:00 AM	
08:30 AM	
09:00 AM	
09:30 AM	
10:00 AM	
10:30 AM	
11:00 AM	
11:30 AM	
12:00 PM	
12:30 PM	
01:00 PM	
01:30 PM	
02:00 PM	
02:30 PM	
03:00 PM	
03:30 PM	
04:00 PM	
04:30 PM	
05:00 PM	
05:30 PM	
06:00 PM	
06:30 PM	
07:00 PM	
07:30 PM	
08:00 PM	
08:30 PM	

TUESDAY
11
Rosh Hashanah Ends

07:00 AM	
07:30 AM	
08:00 AM	
08:30 AM	
09:00 AM	
09:30 AM	
10:00 AM	
10:30 AM	
11:00 AM	
11:30 AM	
12:00 PM	
12:30 PM	
01:00 PM	
01:30 PM	
02:00 PM	
02:30 PM	
03:00 PM	
03:30 PM	
04:00 PM	
04:30 PM	
05:00 PM	
05:30 PM	
06:00 PM	
06:30 PM	
07:00 PM	
07:30 PM	
08:00 PM	
08:30 PM	

WEDNESDAY
12

07:00 AM	
07:30 AM	
08:00 AM	
08:30 AM	
09:00 AM	
09:30 AM	
10:00 AM	
10:30 AM	
11:00 AM	
11:30 AM	
12:00 PM	
12:30 PM	
01:00 PM	
01:30 PM	
02:00 PM	
02:30 PM	
03:00 PM	
03:30 PM	
04:00 PM	
04:30 PM	
05:00 PM	
05:30 PM	
06:00 PM	
06:30 PM	
07:00 PM	
07:30 PM	
08:00 PM	
08:30 PM	

AUGUST 2018
S M T W T F S
1 2 3 4
5 6 7 8 9 10 11
12 13 14 15 16 17 18
19 20 21 22 23 24 25
26 27 28 29 30 31

SEPTEMBER 2018
S M T W T F S
1
2 3 4 5 6 7 8
9 10 11 12 13 14 15
16 17 18 19 20 21 22
23 24 25 26 27 28 29
30

OCTOBER 2018
S M T W T F S
1 2 3 4 5 6
7 8 9 10 11 12 13
14 15 16 17 18 19 20
21 22 23 24 25 26 27
28 29 30 31

SEPTEMBER

THURSDAY 13

07:00 AM
07:30 AM
08:00 AM
08:30 AM
09:00 AM
09:30 AM
10:00 AM
10:30 AM
11:00 AM
11:30 AM
12:00 PM
12:30 PM
01:00 PM
01:30 PM
02:00 PM
02:30 PM
03:00 PM
03:30 PM
04:00 PM
04:30 PM
05:00 PM
05:30 PM
06:00 PM
06:30 PM
07:00 PM
07:30 PM
08:00 PM
08:30 PM

FRIDAY 14

07:00 AM
07:30 AM
08:00 AM
08:30 AM
09:00 AM
09:30 AM
10:00 AM
10:30 AM
11:00 AM
11:30 AM
12:00 PM
12:30 PM
01:00 PM
01:30 PM
02:00 PM
02:30 PM
03:00 PM
03:30 PM
04:00 PM
04:30 PM
05:00 PM
05:30 PM
06:00 PM
06:30 PM
07:00 PM
07:30 PM
08:00 PM
08:30 PM

SATURDAY 15

SUNDAY 16

SEPT

SEPTEMBER

AUGUST 2018
S	M	T	W	T	F	S
			1	2	3	4
5	6	7	8	9	10	11
12	13	14	15	16	17	18
19	20	21	22	23	24	25
26	27	28	29	30	31	

SEPTEMBER 2018
S	M	T	W	T	F	S
						1
2	3	4	5	6	7	8
9	10	11	12	13	14	15
16	17	18	19	20	21	22
23	24	25	26	27	28	29
30						

OCTOBER 2018
S	M	T	W	T	F	S
	1	2	3	4	5	6
7	8	9	10	11	12	13
14	15	16	17	18	19	20
21	22	23	24	25	26	27
28	29	30	31			

Prayer Requests

REFLECTIONS

The ransomed of the Lord will return. They will enter Zion with singing; everlasting joy will crown their heads. Gladness and joy will overtake them, and sorrow and sighing will flee away.

Isaiah 35:10 NIV

SEPT

NOTES

To Do

- [ ]
- [ ]
- [ ]
- [ ]
- [ ]
- [ ]
- [ ]
- [ ]
- [ ]
- [ ]
- [ ]
- [ ]
- [ ]
- [ ]

SEPTEMBER

MONDAY 17	TUESDAY 18 — Yom Kippur Begins	WEDNESDAY 19 — Yom Kippur Ends
07:00 AM	07:00 AM	07:00 AM
07:30 AM	07:30 AM	07:30 AM
08:00 AM	08:00 AM	08:00 AM
08:30 AM	08:30 AM	08:30 AM
09:00 AM	09:00 AM	09:00 AM
09:30 AM	09:30 AM	09:30 AM
10:00 AM	10:00 AM	10:00 AM
10:30 AM	10:30 AM	10:30 AM
11:00 AM	11:00 AM	11:00 AM
11:30 AM	11:30 AM	11:30 AM
12:00 PM	12:00 PM	12:00 PM
12:30 PM	12:30 PM	12:30 PM
01:00 PM	01:00 PM	01:00 PM
01:30 PM	01:30 PM	01:30 PM
02:00 PM	02:00 PM	02:00 PM
02:30 PM	02:30 PM	02:30 PM
03:00 PM	03:00 PM	03:00 PM
03:30 PM	03:30 PM	03:30 PM
04:00 PM	04:00 PM	04:00 PM
04:30 PM	04:30 PM	04:30 PM
05:00 PM	05:00 PM	05:00 PM
05:30 PM	05:30 PM	05:30 PM
06:00 PM	06:00 PM	06:00 PM
06:30 PM	06:30 PM	06:30 PM
07:00 PM	07:00 PM	07:00 PM
07:30 PM	07:30 PM	07:30 PM
08:00 PM	08:00 PM	08:00 PM
08:30 PM	08:30 PM	08:30 PM

SEPT

AUGUST 2018
S	M	T	W	T	F	S
			1	2	3	4
5	6	7	8	9	10	11
12	13	14	15	16	17	18
19	20	21	22	23	24	25
26	27	28	29	30	31	

SEPTEMBER 2018
S	M	T	W	T	F	S
						1
2	3	4	5	6	7	8
9	10	11	12	13	14	15
16	17	18	19	20	21	22
23	24	25	26	27	28	29
30						

OCTOBER 2018
S	M	T	W	T	F	S
	1	2	3	4	5	6
7	8	9	10	11	12	13
14	15	16	17	18	19	20
21	22	23	24	25	26	27
28	29	30	31			

SEPTEMBER

THURSDAY 20

- 07:00 AM
- 07:30 AM
- 08:00 AM
- 08:30 AM
- 09:00 AM
- 09:30 AM
- 10:00 AM
- 10:30 AM
- 11:00 AM
- 11:30 AM
- 12:00 PM
- 12:30 PM
- 01:00 PM
- 01:30 PM
- 02:00 PM
- 02:30 PM
- 03:00 PM
- 03:30 PM
- 04:00 PM
- 04:30 PM
- 05:00 PM
- 05:30 PM
- 06:00 PM
- 06:30 PM
- 07:00 PM
- 07:30 PM
- 08:00 PM
- 08:30 PM

FRIDAY 21

- 07:00 AM
- 07:30 AM
- 08:00 AM
- 08:30 AM
- 09:00 AM
- 09:30 AM
- 10:00 AM
- 10:30 AM
- 11:00 AM
- 11:30 AM
- 12:00 PM
- 12:30 PM
- 01:00 PM
- 01:30 PM
- 02:00 PM
- 02:30 PM
- 03:00 PM
- 03:30 PM
- 04:00 PM
- 04:30 PM
- 05:00 PM
- 05:30 PM
- 06:00 PM
- 06:30 PM
- 07:00 PM
- 07:30 PM
- 08:00 PM
- 08:30 PM

SATURDAY 22

SUNDAY 23
Autumnal Equinox

S E P T

SEPTEMBER

AUGUST 2018
S	M	T	W	T	F	S
			1	2	3	4
5	6	7	8	9	10	11
12	13	14	15	16	17	18
19	20	21	22	23	24	25
26	27	28	29	30	31	

SEPTEMBER 2018
S	M	T	W	T	F	S
						1
2	3	4	5	6	7	8
9	10	11	12	13	14	15
16	17	18	19	20	21	22
23	24	25	26	27	28	29
30						

OCTOBER 2018
S	M	T	W	T	F	S
	1	2	3	4	5	6
7	8	9	10	11	12	13
14	15	16	17	18	19	20
21	22	23	24	25	26	27
28	29	30	31			

Prayer Requests

REFLECTIONS

I consider that the sufferings of this present time are not worth comparing with the glory that is to be revealed to us.

Romans 8:18 ESV

SEPT

NOTES

_____
_____
_____
_____
_____
_____
_____
_____
_____
_____
_____
_____
_____
_____
_____
_____
_____
_____

To Do

- [ ] _____
- [ ] _____
- [ ] _____
- [ ] _____
- [ ] _____
- [ ] _____
- [ ] _____
- [ ] _____
- [ ] _____
- [ ] _____
- [ ] _____
- [ ] _____
- [ ] _____
- [ ] _____
- [ ] _____
- [ ] _____

SEPTEMBER

MONDAY **24**	TUESDAY **25**	WEDNESDAY **26**
07:00 AM	07:00 AM	07:00 AM
07:30 AM	07:30 AM	07:30 AM
08:00 AM	08:00 AM	08:00 AM
08:30 AM	08:30 AM	08:30 AM
09:00 AM	09:00 AM	09:00 AM
09:30 AM	09:30 AM	09:30 AM
10:00 AM	10:00 AM	10:00 AM
10:30 AM	10:30 AM	10:30 AM
11:00 AM	11:00 AM	11:00 AM
11:30 AM	11:30 AM	11:30 AM
12:00 PM	12:00 PM	12:00 PM
12:30 PM	12:30 PM	12:30 PM
01:00 PM	01:00 PM	01:00 PM
01:30 PM	01:30 PM	01:30 PM
02:00 PM	02:00 PM	02:00 PM
02:30 PM	02:30 PM	02:30 PM
03:00 PM	03:00 PM	03:00 PM
03:30 PM	03:30 PM	03:30 PM
04:00 PM	04:00 PM	04:00 PM
04:30 PM	04:30 PM	04:30 PM
05:00 PM	05:00 PM	05:00 PM
05:30 PM	05:30 PM	05:30 PM
06:00 PM	06:00 PM	06:00 PM
06:30 PM	06:30 PM	06:30 PM
07:00 PM	07:00 PM	07:00 PM
07:30 PM	07:30 PM	07:30 PM
08:00 PM	08:00 PM	08:00 PM
08:30 PM	08:30 PM	08:30 PM

AUGUST 2018	SEPTEMBER 2018	OCTOBER 2018
S M T W T F S	S M T W T F S	S M T W T F S
1 2 3 4	1	1 2 3 4 5 6
5 6 7 8 9 10 11	2 3 4 5 6 7 8	7 8 9 10 11 12 13
12 13 14 15 16 17 18	9 10 11 12 13 14 15	14 15 16 17 18 19 20
19 20 21 22 23 24 25	16 17 18 19 20 21 22	21 22 23 24 25 26 27
26 27 28 29 30 31	23 24 25 26 27 28 29	28 29 30 31
	30	

SEPTEMBER

THURSDAY 27

07:00 AM	
07:30 AM	
08:00 AM	
08:30 AM	
09:00 AM	
09:30 AM	
10:00 AM	
10:30 AM	
11:00 AM	
11:30 AM	
12:00 PM	
12:30 PM	
01:00 PM	
01:30 PM	
02:00 PM	
02:30 PM	
03:00 PM	
03:30 PM	
04:00 PM	
04:30 PM	
05:00 PM	
05:30 PM	
06:00 PM	
06:30 PM	
07:00 PM	
07:30 PM	
08:00 PM	
08:30 PM	

FRIDAY 28

07:00 AM	
07:30 AM	
08:00 AM	
08:30 AM	
09:00 AM	
09:30 AM	
10:00 AM	
10:30 AM	
11:00 AM	
11:30 AM	
12:00 PM	
12:30 PM	
01:00 PM	
01:30 PM	
02:00 PM	
02:30 PM	
03:00 PM	
03:30 PM	
04:00 PM	
04:30 PM	
05:00 PM	
05:30 PM	
06:00 PM	
06:30 PM	
07:00 PM	
07:30 PM	
08:00 PM	
08:30 PM	

SATURDAY 29

SUNDAY 30

S
E
P
T

SEPTEMBER

AUGUST 2018

S	M	T	W	T	F	S
			1	2	3	4
5	6	7	8	9	10	11
12	13	14	15	16	17	18
19	20	21	22	23	24	25
26	27	28	29	30	31	

SEPTEMBER 2018

S	M	T	W	T	F	S
						1
2	3	4	5	6	7	8
9	10	11	12	13	14	15
16	17	18	19	20	21	22
23	24	25	26	27	28	29
30						

OCTOBER 2018

S	M	T	W	T	F	S
	1	2	3	4	5	6
7	8	9	10	11	12	13
14	15	16	17	18	19	20
21	22	23	24	25	26	27
28	29	30	31			

Prayer Requests

REFLECTIONS

We can make our plans, but the Lord determines our steps.

Proverbs 16:9 NLT

SEPT

NOTES

To Do

SEPT

OCTOBER

2018

With me are riches and honor,
enduring wealth and prosperity.
My fruit is better than fine gold;
what I yield surpasses choice silver.
I walk in the way of righteousness,
along the paths of justice,
bestowing a rich inheritance
on those who love me
and making their treasuries full.

PROVERBS 8:18-21 NIV

MY GOALS FOR THE MONTH

_____
_____
_____
_____
_____
_____
_____
_____
_____
_____
_____
_____
_____
_____
_____
_____
_____
_____

MONTH AT A GLANCE

MONDAY	1	
TUESDAY	2	
WEDNESDAY	3	
THURSDAY	4	
FRIDAY	5	
SATURDAY	6	
SUNDAY	7	
MONDAY	8	
TUESDAY	9	
WEDNESDAY	10	
THURSDAY	11	
FRIDAY	12	
SATURDAY	13	
SUNDAY	14	
MONDAY	15	
TUESDAY	16	
WEDNESDAY	17	
THURSDAY	18	
FRIDAY	19	
SATURDAY	20	
SUNDAY	21	
MONDAY	22	
TUESDAY	23	
WEDNESDAY	24	
THURSDAY	25	
FRIDAY	26	
SATURDAY	27	
SUNDAY	28	
MONDAY	29	
TUESDAY	30	
WEDNESDAY	31	

OCTOBER

"Nothing is hidden that will not be made manifest, nor is anything secret that will not be known and come to light."

Luke 8:17 ESV

MONDAY 1	TUESDAY 2	WEDNESDAY 3
07:00 AM	07:00 AM	07:00 AM
07:30 AM	07:30 AM	07:30 AM
08:00 AM	08:00 AM	08:00 AM
08:30 AM	08:30 AM	08:30 AM
09:00 AM	09:00 AM	09:00 AM
09:30 AM	09:30 AM	09:30 AM
10:00 AM	10:00 AM	10:00 AM
10:30 AM	10:30 AM	10:30 AM
11:00 AM	11:00 AM	11:00 AM
11:30 AM	11:30 AM	11:30 AM
12:00 PM	12:00 PM	12:00 PM
12:30 PM	12:30 PM	12:30 PM
01:00 PM	01:00 PM	01:00 PM
01:30 PM	01:30 PM	01:30 PM
02:00 PM	02:00 PM	02:00 PM
02:30 PM	02:30 PM	02:30 PM
03:00 PM	03:00 PM	03:00 PM
03:30 PM	03:30 PM	03:30 PM
04:00 PM	04:00 PM	04:00 PM
04:30 PM	04:30 PM	04:30 PM
05:00 PM	05:00 PM	05:00 PM
05:30 PM	05:30 PM	05:30 PM
06:00 PM	06:00 PM	06:00 PM
06:30 PM	06:30 PM	06:30 PM
07:00 PM	07:00 PM	07:00 PM
07:30 PM	07:30 PM	07:30 PM
08:00 PM	08:00 PM	08:00 PM
08:30 PM	08:30 PM	08:30 PM

OCT

SEPTEMBER 2018
S M T W T F S
            1
2 3 4 5 6 7 8
9 10 11 12 13 14 15
16 17 18 19 20 21 22
23 24 25 26 27 28 29
30

OCTOBER 2018
S M T W T F S
    1 2 3 4 5 6
7 8 9 10 11 12 13
14 15 16 17 18 19 20
21 22 23 24 25 26 27
28 29 30 31

NOVEMBER 2018
S M T W T F S
            1 2 3
4 5 6 7 8 9 10
11 12 13 14 15 16 17
18 19 20 21 22 23 24
25 26 27 28 29 30

OCTOBER

THURSDAY
4

07:00 AM	
07:30 AM	
08:00 AM	
08:30 AM	
09:00 AM	
09:30 AM	
10:00 AM	
10:30 AM	
11:00 AM	
11:30 AM	
12:00 PM	
12:30 PM	
01:00 PM	
01:30 PM	
02:00 PM	
02:30 PM	
03:00 PM	
03:30 PM	
04:00 PM	
04:30 PM	
05:00 PM	
05:30 PM	
06:00 PM	
06:30 PM	
07:00 PM	
07:30 PM	
08:00 PM	
08:30 PM	

FRIDAY
5

07:00 AM	
07:30 AM	
08:00 AM	
08:30 AM	
09:00 AM	
09:30 AM	
10:00 AM	
10:30 AM	
11:00 AM	
11:30 AM	
12:00 PM	
12:30 PM	
01:00 PM	
01:30 PM	
02:00 PM	
02:30 PM	
03:00 PM	
03:30 PM	
04:00 PM	
04:30 PM	
05:00 PM	
05:30 PM	
06:00 PM	
06:30 PM	
07:00 PM	
07:30 PM	
08:00 PM	
08:30 PM	

SATURDAY
6

SUNDAY
7

OCTOBER

SEPTEMBER 2018
S	M	T	W	T	F	S
						1
2	3	4	5	6	7	8
9	10	11	12	13	14	15
16	17	18	19	20	21	22
23	24	25	26	27	28	29
30						

OCTOBER 2018
S	M	T	W	T	F	S
	1	2	3	4	5	6
7	8	9	10	11	12	13
14	15	16	17	18	19	20
21	22	23	24	25	26	27
28	29	30	31			

NOVEMBER 2018
S	M	T	W	T	F	S
				1	2	3
4	5	6	7	8	9	10
11	12	13	14	15	16	17
18	19	20	21	22	23	24
25	26	27	28	29	30	

Prayer Requests

REFLECTIONS

Those who deal truthfully are His delight.

Proverbs 12:22 NKJV

OCT

NOTES

To Do

- [ ]
- [ ]
- [ ]
- [ ]
- [ ]
- [ ]
- [ ]
- [ ]
- [ ]
- [ ]
- [ ]
- [ ]
- [ ]
- [ ]
- [ ]

OCTOBER

MONDAY 8 — Columbus Day

07:00 AM	
07:30 AM	
08:00 AM	
08:30 AM	
09:00 AM	
09:30 AM	
10:00 AM	
10:30 AM	
11:00 AM	
11:30 AM	
12:00 PM	
12:30 PM	
01:00 PM	
01:30 PM	
02:00 PM	
02:30 PM	
03:00 PM	
03:30 PM	
04:00 PM	
04:30 PM	
05:00 PM	
05:30 PM	
06:00 PM	
06:30 PM	
07:00 PM	
07:30 PM	
08:00 PM	
08:30 PM	

TUESDAY 9

07:00 AM	
07:30 AM	
08:00 AM	
08:30 AM	
09:00 AM	
09:30 AM	
10:00 AM	
10:30 AM	
11:00 AM	
11:30 AM	
12:00 PM	
12:30 PM	
01:00 PM	
01:30 PM	
02:00 PM	
02:30 PM	
03:00 PM	
03:30 PM	
04:00 PM	
04:30 PM	
05:00 PM	
05:30 PM	
06:00 PM	
06:30 PM	
07:00 PM	
07:30 PM	
08:00 PM	
08:30 PM	

WEDNESDAY 10

07:00 AM	
07:30 AM	
08:00 AM	
08:30 AM	
09:00 AM	
09:30 AM	
10:00 AM	
10:30 AM	
11:00 AM	
11:30 AM	
12:00 PM	
12:30 PM	
01:00 PM	
01:30 PM	
02:00 PM	
02:30 PM	
03:00 PM	
03:30 PM	
04:00 PM	
04:30 PM	
05:00 PM	
05:30 PM	
06:00 PM	
06:30 PM	
07:00 PM	
07:30 PM	
08:00 PM	
08:30 PM	

SEPTEMBER 2018
S	M	T	W	T	F	S
						1
2	3	4	5	6	7	8
9	10	11	12	13	14	15
16	17	18	19	20	21	22
23	24	25	26	27	28	29
30						

OCTOBER 2018
S	M	T	W	T	F	S
	1	2	3	4	5	6
7	8	9	10	11	12	13
14	15	16	17	18	19	20
21	22	23	24	25	26	27
28	29	30	31			

NOVEMBER 2018
S	M	T	W	T	F	S
				1	2	3
4	5	6	7	8	9	10
11	12	13	14	15	16	17
18	19	20	21	22	23	24
25	26	27	28	29	30	

OCTOBER

THURSDAY 11

07:00 AM
07:30 AM
08:00 AM
08:30 AM
09:00 AM
09:30 AM
10:00 AM
10:30 AM
11:00 AM
11:30 AM
12:00 PM
12:30 PM
01:00 PM
01:30 PM
02:00 PM
02:30 PM
03:00 PM
03:30 PM
04:00 PM
04:30 PM
05:00 PM
05:30 PM
06:00 PM
06:30 PM
07:00 PM
07:30 PM
08:00 PM
08:30 PM

FRIDAY 12

07:00 AM
07:30 AM
08:00 AM
08:30 AM
09:00 AM
09:30 AM
10:00 AM
10:30 AM
11:00 AM
11:30 AM
12:00 PM
12:30 PM
01:00 PM
01:30 PM
02:00 PM
02:30 PM
03:00 PM
03:30 PM
04:00 PM
04:30 PM
05:00 PM
05:30 PM
06:00 PM
06:30 PM
07:00 PM
07:30 PM
08:00 PM
08:30 PM

SATURDAY 13

SUNDAY 14

OCT

OCTOBER

SEPTEMBER 2018
S	M	T	W	T	F	S
						1
2	3	4	5	6	7	8
9	10	11	12	13	14	15
16	17	18	19	20	21	22
23	24	25	26	27	28	29
30						

OCTOBER 2018
S	M	T	W	T	F	S
	1	2	3	4	5	6
7	8	9	10	11	12	13
14	15	16	17	18	19	20
21	22	23	24	25	26	27
28	29	30	31			

NOVEMBER 2018
S	M	T	W	T	F	S
				1	2	3
4	5	6	7	8	9	10
11	12	13	14	15	16	17
18	19	20	21	22	23	24
25	26	27	28	29	30	

Prayer Requests

REFLECTIONS

*"My Father will
honor the one who
serves me."*

John 12:26 NIV

OCT

NOTES

_____
_____
_____
_____
_____
_____
_____
_____
_____
_____
_____
_____
_____
_____
_____
_____
_____
_____

To Do

- [ ] _____
- [ ] _____
- [ ] _____
- [ ] _____
- [ ] _____
- [ ] _____
- [ ] _____
- [ ] _____
- [ ] _____
- [ ] _____
- [ ] _____
- [ ] _____
- [ ] _____
- [ ] _____

OCTOBER

OCT

MONDAY **15**	TUESDAY **16**	WEDNESDAY **17**
07:00 AM	07:00 AM	07:00 AM
07:30 AM	07:30 AM	07:30 AM
08:00 AM	08:00 AM	08:00 AM
08:30 AM	08:30 AM	08:30 AM
09:00 AM	09:00 AM	09:00 AM
09:30 AM	09:30 AM	09:30 AM
10:00 AM	10:00 AM	10:00 AM
10:30 AM	10:30 AM	10:30 AM
11:00 AM	11:00 AM	11:00 AM
11:30 AM	11:30 AM	11:30 AM
12:00 PM	12:00 PM	12:00 PM
12:30 PM	12:30 PM	12:30 PM
01:00 PM	01:00 PM	01:00 PM
01:30 PM	01:30 PM	01:30 PM
02:00 PM	02:00 PM	02:00 PM
02:30 PM	02:30 PM	02:30 PM
03:00 PM	03:00 PM	03:00 PM
03:30 PM	03:30 PM	03:30 PM
04:00 PM	04:00 PM	04:00 PM
04:30 PM	04:30 PM	04:30 PM
05:00 PM	05:00 PM	05:00 PM
05:30 PM	05:30 PM	05:30 PM
06:00 PM	06:00 PM	06:00 PM
06:30 PM	06:30 PM	06:30 PM
07:00 PM	07:00 PM	07:00 PM
07:30 PM	07:30 PM	07:30 PM
08:00 PM	08:00 PM	08:00 PM
08:30 PM	08:30 PM	08:30 PM

SEPTEMBER 2018	OCTOBER 2018	NOVEMBER 2018
S M T W T F S	S M T W T F S	S M T W T F S
1	1 2 3 4 5 6	1 2 3
2 3 4 5 6 7 8	7 8 9 10 11 12 13	4 5 6 7 8 9 10
9 10 11 12 13 14 15	14 15 16 17 18 19 20	11 12 13 14 15 16 17
16 17 18 19 20 21 22	21 22 23 24 25 26 27	18 19 20 21 22 23 24
23 24 25 26 27 28 29	28 29 30 31	25 26 27 28 29 30
30		

OCTOBER

THURSDAY 18

07:00 AM
07:30 AM
08:00 AM
08:30 AM
09:00 AM
09:30 AM
10:00 AM
10:30 AM
11:00 AM
11:30 AM
12:00 PM
12:30 PM
01:00 PM
01:30 PM
02:00 PM
02:30 PM
03:00 PM
03:30 PM
04:00 PM
04:30 PM
05:00 PM
05:30 PM
06:00 PM
06:30 PM
07:00 PM
07:30 PM
08:00 PM
08:30 PM

FRIDAY 19

07:00 AM
07:30 AM
08:00 AM
08:30 AM
09:00 AM
09:30 AM
10:00 AM
10:30 AM
11:00 AM
11:30 AM
12:00 PM
12:30 PM
01:00 PM
01:30 PM
02:00 PM
02:30 PM
03:00 PM
03:30 PM
04:00 PM
04:30 PM
05:00 PM
05:30 PM
06:00 PM
06:30 PM
07:00 PM
07:30 PM
08:00 PM
08:30 PM

SATURDAY 20

SUNDAY 21

OCT

OCTOBER

SEPTEMBER 2018
S M T W T F S
1
2 3 4 5 6 7 8
9 10 11 12 13 14 15
16 17 18 19 20 21 22
23 24 25 26 27 28 29
30

OCTOBER 2018
S M T W T F S
1 2 3 4 5 6
7 8 9 10 11 12 13
14 15 16 17 18 19 20
21 22 23 24 25 26 27
28 29 30 31

NOVEMBER 2018
S M T W T F S
1 2 3
4 5 6 7 8 9 10
11 12 13 14 15 16 17
18 19 20 21 22 23 24
25 26 27 28 29 30

Prayer Requests

REFLECTIONS

*The Lord takes
pleasure in those
who fear Him,
In those who hope
in His mercy.*

Psalm 147:11 NKJV

OCT

NOTES

To Do

OCT

OCTOBER

MONDAY 22	TUESDAY 23	WEDNESDAY 24
07:00 AM	07:00 AM	07:00 AM
07:30 AM	07:30 AM	07:30 AM
08:00 AM	08:00 AM	08:00 AM
08:30 AM	08:30 AM	08:30 AM
09:00 AM	09:00 AM	09:00 AM
09:30 AM	09:30 AM	09:30 AM
10:00 AM	10:00 AM	10:00 AM
10:30 AM	10:30 AM	10:30 AM
11:00 AM	11:00 AM	11:00 AM
11:30 AM	11:30 AM	11:30 AM
12:00 PM	12:00 PM	12:00 PM
12:30 PM	12:30 PM	12:30 PM
01:00 PM	01:00 PM	01:00 PM
01:30 PM	01:30 PM	01:30 PM
02:00 PM	02:00 PM	02:00 PM
02:30 PM	02:30 PM	02:30 PM
03:00 PM	03:00 PM	03:00 PM
03:30 PM	03:30 PM	03:30 PM
04:00 PM	04:00 PM	04:00 PM
04:30 PM	04:30 PM	04:30 PM
05:00 PM	05:00 PM	05:00 PM
05:30 PM	05:30 PM	05:30 PM
06:00 PM	06:00 PM	06:00 PM
06:30 PM	06:30 PM	06:30 PM
07:00 PM	07:00 PM	07:00 PM
07:30 PM	07:30 PM	07:30 PM
08:00 PM	08:00 PM	08:00 PM
08:30 PM	08:30 PM	08:30 PM

SEPTEMBER 2018
S M T W T F S
1
2 3 4 5 6 7 8
9 10 11 12 13 14 15
16 17 18 19 20 21 22
23 24 25 26 27 28 29
30

OCTOBER 2018
S M T W T F S
1 2 3 4 5 6
7 8 9 10 11 12 13
14 15 16 17 18 19 20
21 22 23 24 25 26 27
28 29 30 31

NOVEMBER 2018
S M T W T F S
1 2 3
4 5 6 7 8 9 10
11 12 13 14 15 16 17
18 19 20 21 22 23 24
25 26 27 28 29 30

OCTOBER

THURSDAY 25

07:00 AM
07:30 AM
08:00 AM
08:30 AM
09:00 AM
09:30 AM
10:00 AM
10:30 AM
11:00 AM
11:30 AM
12:00 PM
12:30 PM
01:00 PM
01:30 PM
02:00 PM
02:30 PM
03:00 PM
03:30 PM
04:00 PM
04:30 PM
05:00 PM
05:30 PM
06:00 PM
06:30 PM
07:00 PM
07:30 PM
08:00 PM
08:30 PM

FRIDAY 26

07:00 AM
07:30 AM
08:00 AM
08:30 AM
09:00 AM
09:30 AM
10:00 AM
10:30 AM
11:00 AM
11:30 AM
12:00 PM
12:30 PM
01:00 PM
01:30 PM
02:00 PM
02:30 PM
03:00 PM
03:30 PM
04:00 PM
04:30 PM
05:00 PM
05:30 PM
06:00 PM
06:30 PM
07:00 PM
07:30 PM
08:00 PM
08:30 PM

SATURDAY 27

SUNDAY 28

O
C
T

OCTOBER

SEPTEMBER 2018
S M T W T F S
1
2 3 4 5 6 7 8
9 10 11 12 13 14 15
16 17 18 19 20 21 22
23 24 25 26 27 28 29
30

OCTOBER 2018
S M T W T F S
1 2 3 4 5 6
7 8 9 10 11 12 13
14 15 16 17 18 19 20
21 22 23 24 25 26 27
28 29 30 31

NOVEMBER 2018
S M T W T F S
1 2 3
4 5 6 7 8 9 10
11 12 13 14 15 16 17
18 19 20 21 22 23 24
25 26 27 28 29 30

Prayer Requests

REFLECTIONS

*Pride will ruin
people,
but those who
are humble will
be honored.*

Proverbs 29:23
NCV

OCT

NOTES

To Do

NOVEMBER

2018

My child, pay attention to what I say.
Listen carefully to my words.
Don't lose sight of them.
Let them penetrate deep into your heart,
for they bring life to those who find them,
and healing to their whole body.

PROVERBS 4:20-22 NLT

MY GOALS FOR THE MONTH

_____
_____
_____
_____
_____
_____
_____
_____
_____
_____
_____
_____
_____
_____
_____
_____

MONTH AT A GLANCE

THURSDAY	1	
FRIDAY	2	
SATURDAY	3	
SUNDAY	4	
MONDAY	5	
TUESDAY	6	
WEDNESDAY	7	
THURSDAY	8	
FRIDAY	9	
SATURDAY	10	
SUNDAY	11	
MONDAY	12	
TUESDAY	13	
WEDNESDAY	14	
THURSDAY	15	
FRIDAY	16	
SATURDAY	17	
SUNDAY	18	
MONDAY	19	
TUESDAY	20	
WEDNESDAY	21	
THURSDAY	22	
FRIDAY	23	
SATURDAY	24	
SUNDAY	25	
MONDAY	26	
TUESDAY	27	
WEDNESDAY	28	
THURSDAY	29	
FRIDAY	30	

OCTOBER

MONDAY **29**	TUESDAY **30**	WEDNESDAY **31**
07:00 AM	07:00 AM	07:00 AM
07:30 AM	07:30 AM	07:30 AM
08:00 AM	08:00 AM	08:00 AM
08:30 AM	08:30 AM	08:30 AM
09:00 AM	09:00 AM	09:00 AM
09:30 AM	09:30 AM	09:30 AM
10:00 AM	10:00 AM	10:00 AM
10:30 AM	10:30 AM	10:30 AM
11:00 AM	11:00 AM	11:00 AM
11:30 AM	11:30 AM	11:30 AM
12:00 PM	12:00 PM	12:00 PM
12:30 PM	12:30 PM	12:30 PM
01:00 PM	01:00 PM	01:00 PM
01:30 PM	01:30 PM	01:30 PM
02:00 PM	02:00 PM	02:00 PM
02:30 PM	02:30 PM	02:30 PM
03:00 PM	03:00 PM	03:00 PM
03:30 PM	03:30 PM	03:30 PM
04:00 PM	04:00 PM	04:00 PM
04:30 PM	04:30 PM	04:30 PM
05:00 PM	05:00 PM	05:00 PM
05:30 PM	05:30 PM	05:30 PM
06:00 PM	06:00 PM	06:00 PM
06:30 PM	06:30 PM	06:30 PM
07:00 PM	07:00 PM	07:00 PM
07:30 PM	07:30 PM	07:30 PM
08:00 PM	08:00 PM	08:00 PM
08:30 PM	08:30 PM	08:30 PM

OCTOBER 2018
S	M	T	W	T	F	S
	1	2	3	4	5	6
7	8	9	10	11	12	13
14	15	16	17	18	19	20
21	22	23	24	25	26	27
28	29	30	31			

NOVEMBER 2018
S	M	T	W	T	F	S
				1	2	3
4	5	6	7	8	9	10
11	12	13	14	15	16	17
18	19	20	21	22	23	24
25	26	27	28	29	30	

DECEMBER 2018
S	M	T	W	T	F	S
						1
2	3	4	5	6	7	8
9	10	11	12	13	14	15
16	17	18	19	20	21	22
23	24	25	26	27	28	29
30	31					

NOVEMBER

THURSDAY 1

07:00 AM
07:30 AM
08:00 AM
08:30 AM
09:00 AM
09:30 AM
10:00 AM
10:30 AM
11:00 AM
11:30 AM
12:00 PM
12:30 PM
01:00 PM
01:30 PM
02:00 PM
02:30 PM
03:00 PM
03:30 PM
04:00 PM
04:30 PM
05:00 PM
05:30 PM
06:00 PM
06:30 PM
07:00 PM
07:30 PM
08:00 PM
08:30 PM

FRIDAY 2

07:00 AM
07:30 AM
08:00 AM
08:30 AM
09:00 AM
09:30 AM
10:00 AM
10:30 AM
11:00 AM
11:30 AM
12:00 PM
12:30 PM
01:00 PM
01:30 PM
02:00 PM
02:30 PM
03:00 PM
03:30 PM
04:00 PM
04:30 PM
05:00 PM
05:30 PM
06:00 PM
06:30 PM
07:00 PM
07:30 PM
08:00 PM
08:30 PM

SATURDAY 3

SUNDAY 4

Daylight Saving Time ends

NOVEMBER

OCTOBER 2018
S	M	T	W	T	F	S
	1	2	3	4	5	6
7	8	9	10	11	12	13
14	15	16	17	18	19	20
21	22	23	24	25	26	27
28	29	30	31			

NOVEMBER 2018
S	M	T	W	T	F	S
				1	2	3
4	5	6	7	8	9	10
11	12	13	14	15	16	17
18	19	20	21	22	23	24
25	26	27	28	29	30	

DECEMBER 2018
S	M	T	W	T	F	S
						1
2	3	4	5	6	7	8
9	10	11	12	13	14	15
16	17	18	19	20	21	22
23	24	25	26	27	28	29
30	31					

Prayer Requests

REFLECTIONS

Your laws are my treasure; they are my heart's delight.

Psalm 119:111
NLT

NOV

NOTES

To Do

- [ ]
- [ ]
- [ ]
- [ ]
- [ ]
- [ ]
- [ ]
- [ ]
- [ ]
- [ ]
- [ ]
- [ ]
- [ ]
- [ ]
- [ ]

NOVEMBER

MONDAY 5	TUESDAY 6 — Election Day	WEDNESDAY 7
07:00 AM	07:00 AM	07:00 AM
07:30 AM	07:30 AM	07:30 AM
08:00 AM	08:00 AM	08:00 AM
08:30 AM	08:30 AM	08:30 AM
09:00 AM	09:00 AM	09:00 AM
09:30 AM	09:30 AM	09:30 AM
10:00 AM	10:00 AM	10:00 AM
10:30 AM	10:30 AM	10:30 AM
11:00 AM	11:00 AM	11:00 AM
11:30 AM	11:30 AM	11:30 AM
12:00 PM	12:00 PM	12:00 PM
12:30 PM	12:30 PM	12:30 PM
01:00 PM	01:00 PM	01:00 PM
01:30 PM	01:30 PM	01:30 PM
02:00 PM	02:00 PM	02:00 PM
02:30 PM	02:30 PM	02:30 PM
03:00 PM	03:00 PM	03:00 PM
03:30 PM	03:30 PM	03:30 PM
04:00 PM	04:00 PM	04:00 PM
04:30 PM	04:30 PM	04:30 PM
05:00 PM	05:00 PM	05:00 PM
05:30 PM	05:30 PM	05:30 PM
06:00 PM	06:00 PM	06:00 PM
06:30 PM	06:30 PM	06:30 PM
07:00 PM	07:00 PM	07:00 PM
07:30 PM	07:30 PM	07:30 PM
08:00 PM	08:00 PM	08:00 PM
08:30 PM	08:30 PM	08:30 PM

NOV

OCTOBER 2018
S	M	T	W	T	F	S
	1	2	3	4	5	6
7	8	9	10	11	12	13
14	15	16	17	18	19	20
21	22	23	24	25	26	27
28	29	30	31			

NOVEMBER 2018
S	M	T	W	T	F	S
				1	2	3
4	5	6	7	8	9	10
11	12	13	14	15	16	17
18	19	20	21	22	23	24
25	26	27	28	29	30	

DECEMBER 2018
S	M	T	W	T	F	S
						1
2	3	4	5	6	7	8
9	10	11	12	13	14	15
16	17	18	19	20	21	22
23	24	25	26	27	28	29
30	31					

NOVEMBER

THURSDAY 8

- 07:00 AM
- 07:30 AM
- 08:00 AM
- 08:30 AM
- 09:00 AM
- 09:30 AM
- 10:00 AM
- 10:30 AM
- 11:00 AM
- 11:30 AM
- 12:00 PM
- 12:30 PM
- 01:00 PM
- 01:30 PM
- 02:00 PM
- 02:30 PM
- 03:00 PM
- 03:30 PM
- 04:00 PM
- 04:30 PM
- 05:00 PM
- 05:30 PM
- 06:00 PM
- 06:30 PM
- 07:00 PM
- 07:30 PM
- 08:00 PM
- 08:30 PM

FRIDAY 9

- 07:00 AM
- 07:30 AM
- 08:00 AM
- 08:30 AM
- 09:00 AM
- 09:30 AM
- 10:00 AM
- 10:30 AM
- 11:00 AM
- 11:30 AM
- 12:00 PM
- 12:30 PM
- 01:00 PM
- 01:30 PM
- 02:00 PM
- 02:30 PM
- 03:00 PM
- 03:30 PM
- 04:00 PM
- 04:30 PM
- 05:00 PM
- 05:30 PM
- 06:00 PM
- 06:30 PM
- 07:00 PM
- 07:30 PM
- 08:00 PM
- 08:30 PM

SATURDAY 10

SUNDAY 11
Veterans' Day

N
O
V

NOVEMBER

OCTOBER 2018
S	M	T	W	T	F	S
	1	2	3	4	5	6
7	8	9	10	11	12	13
14	15	16	17	18	19	20
21	22	23	24	25	26	27
28	29	30	31			

NOVEMBER 2018
S	M	T	W	T	F	S
				1	2	3
4	5	6	7	8	9	10
11	12	13	14	15	16	17
18	19	20	21	22	23	24
25	26	27	28	29	30	

DECEMBER 2018
S	M	T	W	T	F	S
						1
2	3	4	5	6	7	8
9	10	11	12	13	14	15
16	17	18	19	20	21	22
23	24	25	26	27	28	29
30	31					

Prayer Requests

REFLECTIONS

Because of my integrity you uphold me and set me in your presence forever.

Psalm 41:12 NIV

NOV

NOTES

To Do

NOVEMBER

MONDAY 12	TUESDAY 13	WEDNESDAY 14
07:00 AM	07:00 AM	07:00 AM
07:30 AM	07:30 AM	07:30 AM
08:00 AM	08:00 AM	08:00 AM
08:30 AM	08:30 AM	08:30 AM
09:00 AM	09:00 AM	09:00 AM
09:30 AM	09:30 AM	09:30 AM
10:00 AM	10:00 AM	10:00 AM
10:30 AM	10:30 AM	10:30 AM
11:00 AM	11:00 AM	11:00 AM
11:30 AM	11:30 AM	11:30 AM
12:00 PM	12:00 PM	12:00 PM
12:30 PM	12:30 PM	12:30 PM
01:00 PM	01:00 PM	01:00 PM
01:30 PM	01:30 PM	01:30 PM
02:00 PM	02:00 PM	02:00 PM
02:30 PM	02:30 PM	02:30 PM
03:00 PM	03:00 PM	03:00 PM
03:30 PM	03:30 PM	03:30 PM
04:00 PM	04:00 PM	04:00 PM
04:30 PM	04:30 PM	04:30 PM
05:00 PM	05:00 PM	05:00 PM
05:30 PM	05:30 PM	05:30 PM
06:00 PM	06:00 PM	06:00 PM
06:30 PM	06:30 PM	06:30 PM
07:00 PM	07:00 PM	07:00 PM
07:30 PM	07:30 PM	07:30 PM
08:00 PM	08:00 PM	08:00 PM
08:30 PM	08:30 PM	08:30 PM

OCTOBER 2018
S	M	T	W	T	F	S
	1	2	3	4	5	6
7	8	9	10	11	12	13
14	15	16	17	18	19	20
21	22	23	24	25	26	27
28	29	30	31			

NOVEMBER 2018
S	M	T	W	T	F	S
				1	2	3
4	5	6	7	8	9	10
11	12	13	14	15	16	17
18	19	20	21	22	23	24
25	26	27	28	29	30	

DECEMBER 2018
S	M	T	W	T	F	S
						1
2	3	4	5	6	7	8
9	10	11	12	13	14	15
16	17	18	19	20	21	22
23	24	25	26	27	28	29
30	31					

NOVEMBER

THURSDAY 15

- 07:00 AM
- 07:30 AM
- 08:00 AM
- 08:30 AM
- 09:00 AM
- 09:30 AM
- 10:00 AM
- 10:30 AM
- 11:00 AM
- 11:30 AM
- 12:00 PM
- 12:30 PM
- 01:00 PM
- 01:30 PM
- 02:00 PM
- 02:30 PM
- 03:00 PM
- 03:30 PM
- 04:00 PM
- 04:30 PM
- 05:00 PM
- 05:30 PM
- 06:00 PM
- 06:30 PM
- 07:00 PM
- 07:30 PM
- 08:00 PM
- 08:30 PM

FRIDAY 16

- 07:00 AM
- 07:30 AM
- 08:00 AM
- 08:30 AM
- 09:00 AM
- 09:30 AM
- 10:00 AM
- 10:30 AM
- 11:00 AM
- 11:30 AM
- 12:00 PM
- 12:30 PM
- 01:00 PM
- 01:30 PM
- 02:00 PM
- 02:30 PM
- 03:00 PM
- 03:30 PM
- 04:00 PM
- 04:30 PM
- 05:00 PM
- 05:30 PM
- 06:00 PM
- 06:30 PM
- 07:00 PM
- 07:30 PM
- 08:00 PM
- 08:30 PM

SATURDAY 17

SUNDAY 18

NOVEMBER

| OCTOBER 2018 | | | | | | |
S	M	T	W	T	F	S
	1	2	3	4	5	6
7	8	9	10	11	12	13
14	15	16	17	18	19	20
21	22	23	24	25	26	27
28	29	30	31			

| NOVEMBER 2018 | | | | | | |
S	M	T	W	T	F	S
				1	2	3
4	5	6	7	8	9	10
11	12	13	14	15	16	17
18	19	20	21	22	23	24
25	26	27	28	29	30	

| DECEMBER 2018 | | | | | | |
S	M	T	W	T	F	S
						1
2	3 ·	4	5	6	7	8
9	10	11	12	13	14	15
16	17	18	19	20	21	22
23	24	25	26	27	28	29
30	31					

Prayer Requests

REFLECTIONS

*You will go out
with joy and be
led out in peace.
The mountains
and hills will
burst into song
before you, and
all the trees in
the fields will
clap their hands.*

Isaiah 55:12 NCV

NOV

NOTES

To Do

- [ ]
- [ ]
- [ ]
- [ ]
- [ ]
- [ ]
- [ ]
- [ ]
- [ ]
- [ ]
- [ ]
- [ ]
- [ ]
- [ ]
- [ ]

NOVEMBER

The LORD secures justice for the poor and upholds the cause of the needy.

Psalm 140:12 NIV

MONDAY 19	TUESDAY 20	WEDNESDAY 21
07:00 AM	07:00 AM	07:00 AM
07:30 AM	07:30 AM	07:30 AM
08:00 AM	08:00 AM	08:00 AM
08:30 AM	08:30 AM	08:30 AM
09:00 AM	09:00 AM	09:00 AM
09:30 AM	09:30 AM	09:30 AM
10:00 AM	10:00 AM	10:00 AM
10:30 AM	10:30 AM	10:30 AM
11:00 AM	11:00 AM	11:00 AM
11:30 AM	11:30 AM	11:30 AM
12:00 PM	12:00 PM	12:00 PM
12:30 PM	12:30 PM	12:30 PM
01:00 PM	01:00 PM	01:00 PM
01:30 PM	01:30 PM	01:30 PM
02:00 PM	02:00 PM	02:00 PM
02:30 PM	02:30 PM	02:30 PM
03:00 PM	03:00 PM	03:00 PM
03:30 PM	03:30 PM	03:30 PM
04:00 PM	04:00 PM	04:00 PM
04:30 PM	04:30 PM	04:30 PM
05:00 PM	05:00 PM	05:00 PM
05:30 PM	05:30 PM	05:30 PM
06:00 PM	06:00 PM	06:00 PM
06:30 PM	06:30 PM	06:30 PM
07:00 PM	07:00 PM	07:00 PM
07:30 PM	07:30 PM	07:30 PM
08:00 PM	08:00 PM	08:00 PM
08:30 PM	08:30 PM	08:30 PM

NOV

OCTOBER 2018
S	M	T	W	T	F	S
	1	2	3	4	5	6
7	8	9	10	11	12	13
14	15	16	17	18	19	20
21	22	23	24	25	26	27
28	29	30	31

NOVEMBER 2018
S	M	T	W	T	F	S
				1	2	3
4	5	6	7	8	9	10
11	12	13	14	15	16	17
18	19	20	21	22	23	24
25	26	27	28	29	30

DECEMBER 2018
S	M	T	W	T	F	S
						1
2	3	4	5	6	7	8
9	10	11	12	13	14	15
16	17	18	19	20	21	22
23	24	25	26	27	28	29
30	31

NOVEMBER

THURSDAY 22
Thanksgiving Day

07:00 AM
07:30 AM
08:00 AM
08:30 AM
09:00 AM
09:30 AM
10:00 AM
10:30 AM
11:00 AM
11:30 AM
12:00 PM
12:30 PM
01:00 PM
01:30 PM
02:00 PM
02:30 PM
03:00 PM
03:30 PM
04:00 PM
04:30 PM
05:00 PM
05:30 PM
06:00 PM
06:30 PM
07:00 PM
07:30 PM
08:00 PM
08:30 PM

FRIDAY 23

07:00 AM
07:30 AM
08:00 AM
08:30 AM
09:00 AM
09:30 AM
10:00 AM
10:30 AM
11:00 AM
11:30 AM
12:00 PM
12:30 PM
01:00 PM
01:30 PM
02:00 PM
02:30 PM
03:00 PM
03:30 PM
04:00 PM
04:30 PM
05:00 PM
05:30 PM
06:00 PM
06:30 PM
07:00 PM
07:30 PM
08:00 PM
08:30 PM

SATURDAY 24

SUNDAY 25

NOV

NOVEMBER

OCTOBER 2018

S	M	T	W	T	F	S
	1	2	3	4	5	6
7	8	9	10	11	12	13
14	15	16	17	18	19	20
21	22	23	24	25	26	27
28	29	30	31			

NOVEMBER 2018

S	M	T	W	T	F	S
				1	2	3
4	5	6	7	8	9	10
11	12	13	14	15	16	17
18	19	20	21	22	23	24
25	26	27	28	29	30	

DECEMBER 2018

S	M	T	W	T	F	S
						1
2	3	4	5	6	7	8
9	10	11	12	13	14	15
16	17	18	19	20	21	22
23	24	25	26	27	28	29
30	31					

Prayer Requests

REFLECTIONS

Righteousness and justice are the foundation of your throne.

Psalm 89:14 NIV

NOV

NOTES

To Do

NOVEMBER

MONDAY 26	TUESDAY 27	WEDNESDAY 28
07:00 AM	07:00 AM	07:00 AM
07:30 AM	07:30 AM	07:30 AM
08:00 AM	08:00 AM	08:00 AM
08:30 AM	08:30 AM	08:30 AM
09:00 AM	09:00 AM	09:00 AM
09:30 AM	09:30 AM	09:30 AM
10:00 AM	10:00 AM	10:00 AM
10:30 AM	10:30 AM	10:30 AM
11:00 AM	11:00 AM	11:00 AM
11:30 AM	11:30 AM	11:30 AM
12:00 PM	12:00 PM	12:00 PM
12:30 PM	12:30 PM	12:30 PM
01:00 PM	01:00 PM	01:00 PM
01:30 PM	01:30 PM	01:30 PM
02:00 PM	02:00 PM	02:00 PM
02:30 PM	02:30 PM	02:30 PM
03:00 PM	03:00 PM	03:00 PM
03:30 PM	03:30 PM	03:30 PM
04:00 PM	04:00 PM	04:00 PM
04:30 PM	04:30 PM	04:30 PM
05:00 PM	05:00 PM	05:00 PM
05:30 PM	05:30 PM	05:30 PM
06:00 PM	06:00 PM	06:00 PM
06:30 PM	06:30 PM	06:30 PM
07:00 PM	07:00 PM	07:00 PM
07:30 PM	07:30 PM	07:30 PM
08:00 PM	08:00 PM	08:00 PM
08:30 PM	08:30 PM	08:30 PM

NOV

OCTOBER 2018	NOVEMBER 2018	DECEMBER 2018
S M T W T F S	S M T W T F S	S M T W T F S
1 2 3 4 5 6	1 2 3	1
7 8 9 10 11 12 13	4 5 6 7 8 9 10	2 3 4 5 6 7 8
14 15 16 17 18 19 20	11 12 13 14 15 16 17	9 10 11 12 13 14 15
21 22 23 24 25 26 27	18 19 20 21 22 23 24	16 17 18 19 20 21 22
28 29 30 31	25 26 27 28 29 30	23 24 25 26 27 28 29
		30 31

DECEMBER

THURSDAY 29

07:00 AM
07:30 AM
08:00 AM
08:30 AM
09:00 AM
09:30 AM
10:00 AM
10:30 AM
11:00 AM
11:30 AM
12:00 PM
12:30 PM
01:00 PM
01:30 PM
02:00 PM
02:30 PM
03:00 PM
03:30 PM
04:00 PM
04:30 PM
05:00 PM
05:30 PM
06:00 PM
06:30 PM
07:00 PM
07:30 PM
08:00 PM
08:30 PM

FRIDAY 30

07:00 AM
07:30 AM
08:00 AM
08:30 AM
09:00 AM
09:30 AM
10:00 AM
10:30 AM
11:00 AM
11:30 AM
12:00 PM
12:30 PM
01:00 PM
01:30 PM
02:00 PM
02:30 PM
03:00 PM
03:30 PM
04:00 PM
04:30 PM
05:00 PM
05:30 PM
06:00 PM
06:30 PM
07:00 PM
07:30 PM
08:00 PM
08:30 PM

SATURDAY 1

SUNDAY 2

First Sunday
of Advent
Hanukkah begins

NOVEMBER

OCTOBER 2018
S	M	T	W	T	F	S
	1	2	3	4	5	6
7	8	9	10	11	12	13
14	15	16	17	18	19	20
21	22	23	24	25	26	27
28	29	30	31			

NOVEMBER 2018
S	M	T	W	T	F	S
				1	2	3
4	5	6	7	8	9	10
11	12	13	14	15	16	17
18	19	20	21	22	23	24
25	26	27	28	29	30	

DECEMBER 2018
S	M	T	W	T	F	S
						1
2	3	4	5	6	7	8
9	10	11	12	13	14	15
16	17	18	19	20	21	22
23	24	25	26	27	28	29
30	31					

Prayer Requests

REFLECTIONS

*The Lord is coming
to judge the earth.
He will judge the
world with justice,
and the nations
with fairness.*

Psalm 98:9 NLT

N
O
V

NOTES

To Do

NOV

DECEMBER

2018

"You are the light of the world. A city set on a hill cannot be hidden. Nor do people light a lamp and put it under a basket, but on a stand, and it gives light to all in the house. In the same way, let your light shine before others, so that they may see your good works and give glory to your Father who is in heaven."

MATTHEW 5:14-16 ESV

MY GOALS FOR THE MONTH

MONTH AT A GLANCE

SATURDAY	1	
SUNDAY	2	
MONDAY	3	
TUESDAY	4	
WEDNESDAY	5	
THURSDAY	6	
FRIDAY	7	
SATURDAY	8	
SUNDAY	9	
MONDAY	10	
TUESDAY	11	
WEDNESDAY	12	
THURSDAY	13	
FRIDAY	14	
SATURDAY	15	
SUNDAY	16	
MONDAY	17	
TUESDAY	18	
WEDNESDAY	19	
THURSDAY	20	
FRIDAY	21	
SATURDAY	22	
SUNDAY	23	
MONDAY	24	
TUESDAY	25	
WEDNESDAY	26	
THURSDAY	27	
FRIDAY	28	
SATURDAY	29	
SUNDAY	30	
MONDAY	31	

DECEMBER

MONDAY
3

07:00 AM
07:30 AM
08:00 AM
08:30 AM
09:00 AM
09:30 AM
10:00 AM
10:30 AM
11:00 AM
11:30 AM
12:00 PM
12:30 PM
01:00 PM
01:30 PM
02:00 PM
02:30 PM
03:00 PM
03:30 PM
04:00 PM
04:30 PM
05:00 PM
05:30 PM
06:00 PM
06:30 PM
07:00 PM
07:30 PM
08:00 PM
08:30 PM

TUESDAY
4

07:00 AM
07:30 AM
08:00 AM
08:30 AM
09:00 AM
09:30 AM
10:00 AM
10:30 AM
11:00 AM
11:30 AM
12:00 PM
12:30 PM
01:00 PM
01:30 PM
02:00 PM
02:30 PM
03:00 PM
03:30 PM
04:00 PM
04:30 PM
05:00 PM
05:30 PM
06:00 PM
06:30 PM
07:00 PM
07:30 PM
08:00 PM
08:30 PM

WEDNESDAY
5

07:00 AM
07:30 AM
08:00 AM
08:30 AM
09:00 AM
09:30 AM
10:00 AM
10:30 AM
11:00 AM
11:30 AM
12:00 PM
12:30 PM
01:00 PM
01:30 PM
02:00 PM
02:30 PM
03:00 PM
03:30 PM
04:00 PM
04:30 PM
05:00 PM
05:30 PM
06:00 PM
06:30 PM
07:00 PM
07:30 PM
08:00 PM
08:30 PM

DEC

NOVEMBER 2018

S	M	T	W	T	F	S
				1	2	3
4	5	6	7	8	9	10
11	12	13	14	15	16	17
18	19	20	21	22	23	24
25	26	27	28	29	30	

DECEMBER 2018

S	M	T	W	T	F	S
						1
2	3	4	5	6	7	8
9	10	11	12	13	14	15
16	17	18	19	20	21	22
23	24	25	26	27	28	29
30	31					

JANUARY 2019

S	M	T	W	T	F	S
		1	2	3	4	5
6	7	8	9	10	11	12
13	14	15	16	17	18	19
20	21	22	23	24	25	26
27	28	29	30	31		

DECEMBER

THURSDAY 6

07:00 AM
07:30 AM
08:00 AM
08:30 AM
09:00 AM
09:30 AM
10:00 AM
10:30 AM
11:00 AM
11:30 AM
12:00 PM
12:30 PM
01:00 PM
01:30 PM
02:00 PM
02:30 PM
03:00 PM
03:30 PM
04:00 PM
04:30 PM
05:00 PM
05:30 PM
06:00 PM
06:30 PM
07:00 PM
07:30 PM
08:00 PM
08:30 PM

FRIDAY 7

07:00 AM
07:30 AM
08:00 AM
08:30 AM
09:00 AM
09:30 AM
10:00 AM
10:30 AM
11:00 AM
11:30 AM
12:00 PM
12:30 PM
01:00 PM
01:30 PM
02:00 PM
02:30 PM
03:00 PM
03:30 PM
04:00 PM
04:30 PM
05:00 PM
05:30 PM
06:00 PM
06:30 PM
07:00 PM
07:30 PM
08:00 PM
08:30 PM

SATURDAY 8

SUNDAY 9

DECEMBER

NOVEMBER 2018
S M T W T F S
1 2 3
4 5 6 7 8 9 10
11 12 13 14 15 16 17
18 19 20 21 22 23 24
25 26 27 28 29 30

DECEMBER 2018
S M T W T F S
1
2 3 4 5 6 7 8
9 10 11 12 13 14 15
16 17 18 19 20 21 22
23 24 25 26 27 28 29
30 31

JANUARY 2019
S M T W T F S
1 2 3 4 5
6 7 8 9 10 11 12
13 14 15 16 17 18 19
20 21 22 23 24 25 26
27 28 29 30 31

Prayer Requests

REFLECTIONS

"Love your
enemies, and
do good, and
lend, expecting
nothing in return,
and your reward
will be great,
and you will be
sons of the Most
High."

Luke 6:35 ESV

DEC

NOTES

_____
_____
_____
_____
_____
_____
_____
_____
_____
_____
_____
_____
_____
_____
_____
_____
_____

To Do

- [ ] _____
- [ ] _____
- [ ] _____
- [ ] _____
- [ ] _____
- [ ] _____
- [ ] _____
- [ ] _____
- [ ] _____
- [ ] _____
- [ ] _____
- [ ] _____
- [ ] _____
- [ ] _____
- [ ] _____

DECEMBER

"Come to me, all you who are weary and burdened, and I will give you rest."

Matthew 11:28 NIV

MONDAY 10 Hanukkah ends	TUESDAY 11	WEDNESDAY 12
07:00 AM	07:00 AM	07:00 AM
07:30 AM	07:30 AM	07:30 AM
08:00 AM	08:00 AM	08:00 AM
08:30 AM	08:30 AM	08:30 AM
09:00 AM	09:00 AM	09:00 AM
09:30 AM	09:30 AM	09:30 AM
10:00 AM	10:00 AM	10:00 AM
10:30 AM	10:30 AM	10:30 AM
11:00 AM	11:00 AM	11:00 AM
11:30 AM	11:30 AM	11:30 AM
12:00 PM	12:00 PM	12:00 PM
12:30 PM	12:30 PM	12:30 PM
01:00 PM	01:00 PM	01:00 PM
01:30 PM	01:30 PM	01:30 PM
02:00 PM	02:00 PM	02:00 PM
02:30 PM	02:30 PM	02:30 PM
03:00 PM	03:00 PM	03:00 PM
03:30 PM	03:30 PM	03:30 PM
04:00 PM	04:00 PM	04:00 PM
04:30 PM	04:30 PM	04:30 PM
05:00 PM	05:00 PM	05:00 PM
05:30 PM	05:30 PM	05:30 PM
06:00 PM	06:00 PM	06:00 PM
06:30 PM	06:30 PM	06:30 PM
07:00 PM	07:00 PM	07:00 PM
07:30 PM	07:30 PM	07:30 PM
08:00 PM	08:00 PM	08:00 PM
08:30 PM	08:30 PM	08:30 PM

DEC

NOVEMBER 2018

S	M	T	W	T	F	S
				1	2	3
4	5	6	7	8	9	10
11	12	13	14	15	16	17
18	19	20	21	22	23	24
25	26	27	28	29	30	

DECEMBER 2018

S	M	T	W	T	F	S
						1
2	3	4	5	6	7	8
9	10	11	12	13	14	15
16	17	18	19	20	21	22
23	24	25	26	27	28	29
30	31					

JANUARY 2019

S	M	T	W	T	F	S
		1	2	3	4	5
6	7	8	9	10	11	12
13	14	15	16	17	18	19
20	21	22	23	24	25	26
27	28	29	30	31		

DECEMBER

THURSDAY 13

07:00 AM
07:30 AM
08:00 AM
08:30 AM
09:00 AM
09:30 AM
10:00 AM
10:30 AM
11:00 AM
11:30 AM
12:00 PM
12:30 PM
01:00 PM
01:30 PM
02:00 PM
02:30 PM
03:00 PM
03:30 PM
04:00 PM
04:30 PM
05:00 PM
05:30 PM
06:00 PM
06:30 PM
07:00 PM
07:30 PM
08:00 PM
08:30 PM

FRIDAY 14

07:00 AM
07:30 AM
08:00 AM
08:30 AM
09:00 AM
09:30 AM
10:00 AM
10:30 AM
11:00 AM
11:30 AM
12:00 PM
12:30 PM
01:00 PM
01:30 PM
02:00 PM
02:30 PM
03:00 PM
03:30 PM
04:00 PM
04:30 PM
05:00 PM
05:30 PM
06:00 PM
06:30 PM
07:00 PM
07:30 PM
08:00 PM
08:30 PM

SATURDAY 15

SUNDAY 16

DECEMBER

NOVEMBER 2018
S M T W T F S
          1 2 3
4 5 6 7 8 9 10
11 12 13 14 15 16 17
18 19 20 21 22 23 24
25 26 27 28 29 30

DECEMBER 2018
S M T W T F S
                1
2 3 4 5 6 7 8
9 10 11 12 13 14 15
16 17 18 19 20 21 22
23 24 25 26 27 28 29
30 31

JANUARY 2019
S M T W T F S
       1 2 3 4 5
6 7 8 9 10 11 12
13 14 15 16 17 18 19
20 21 22 23 24 25 26
27 28 29 30 31

Prayer Requests

REFLECTIONS

*Satisfy us in the
morning with your
unfailing love,
that we may sing
for joy and be glad
all our days.*

Psalm 90:14 NIV

DEC

NOTES

To Do

- [ ]
- [ ]
- [ ]
- [ ]
- [ ]
- [ ]
- [ ]
- [ ]
- [ ]
- [ ]
- [ ]
- [ ]
- [ ]
- [ ]

DECEMBER

Three things will last forever—
faith, hope, and love—
and the greatest of these is love.

1 Corinthians 13:13 NLT

MONDAY 17	TUESDAY 18	WEDNESDAY 19
07:00 AM	07:00 AM	07:00 AM
07:30 AM	07:30 AM	07:30 AM
08:00 AM	08:00 AM	08:00 AM
08:30 AM	08:30 AM	08:30 AM
09:00 AM	09:00 AM	09:00 AM
09:30 AM	09:30 AM	09:30 AM
10:00 AM	10:00 AM	10:00 AM
10:30 AM	10:30 AM	10:30 AM
11:00 AM	11:00 AM	11:00 AM
11:30 AM	11:30 AM	11:30 AM
12:00 PM	12:00 PM	12:00 PM
12:30 PM	12:30 PM	12:30 PM
01:00 PM	01:00 PM	01:00 PM
01:30 PM	01:30 PM	01:30 PM
02:00 PM	02:00 PM	02:00 PM
02:30 PM	02:30 PM	02:30 PM
03:00 PM	03:00 PM	03:00 PM
03:30 PM	03:30 PM	03:30 PM
04:00 PM	04:00 PM	04:00 PM
04:30 PM	04:30 PM	04:30 PM
05:00 PM	05:00 PM	05:00 PM
05:30 PM	05:30 PM	05:30 PM
06:00 PM	06:00 PM	06:00 PM
06:30 PM	06:30 PM	06:30 PM
07:00 PM	07:00 PM	07:00 PM
07:30 PM	07:30 PM	07:30 PM
08:00 PM	08:00 PM	08:00 PM
08:30 PM	08:30 PM	08:30 PM

NOVEMBER 2018

S	M	T	W	T	F	S
				1	2	3
4	5	6	7	8	9	10
11	12	13	14	15	16	17
18	19	20	21	22	23	24
25	26	27	28	29	30	

DECEMBER 2018

S	M	T	W	T	F	S
						1
2	3	4	5	6	7	8
9	10	11	12	13	14	15
16	17	18	19	20	21	22
23	24	25	26	27	28	29
30	31					

JANUARY 2019

S	M	T	W	T	F	S
		1	2	3	4	5
6	7	8	9	10	11	12
13	14	15	16	17	18	19
20	21	22	23	24	25	26
27	28	29	30	31		

DECEMBER

THURSDAY 20

07:00 AM
07:30 AM
08:00 AM
08:30 AM
09:00 AM
09:30 AM
10:00 AM
10:30 AM
11:00 AM
11:30 AM
12:00 PM
12:30 PM
01:00 PM
01:30 PM
02:00 PM
02:30 PM
03:00 PM
03:30 PM
04:00 PM
04:30 PM
05:00 PM
05:30 PM
06:00 PM
06:30 PM
07:00 PM
07:30 PM
08:00 PM
08:30 PM

FRIDAY 21

Winter Solstice

07:00 AM
07:30 AM
08:00 AM
08:30 AM
09:00 AM
09:30 AM
10:00 AM
10:30 AM
11:00 AM
11:30 AM
12:00 PM
12:30 PM
01:00 PM
01:30 PM
02:00 PM
02:30 PM
03:00 PM
03:30 PM
04:00 PM
04:30 PM
05:00 PM
05:30 PM
06:00 PM
06:30 PM
07:00 PM
07:30 PM
08:00 PM
08:30 PM

SATURDAY 22

SUNDAY 23

DEC

DECEMBER

NOVEMBER 2018
S	M	T	W	T	F	S
				1	2	3
4	5	6	7	8	9	10
11	12	13	14	15	16	17
18	19	20	21	22	23	24
25	26	27	28	29	30	

DECEMBER 2018
S	M	T	W	T	F	S
						1
2	3	4	5	6	7	8
9	10	11	12	13	14	15
16	17	18	19	20	21	22
23	24	25	26	27	28	29
30	31					

JANUARY 2019
S	M	T	W	T	F	S
		1	2	3	4	5
6	7	8	9	10	11	12
13	14	15	16	17	18	19
20	21	22	23	24	25	26
27	28	29	30	31		

Prayer Requests

REFLECTIONS

They who wait for the Lord shall renew their strength; they shall mount up with wings like eagles; they shall run and not be weary; they shall walk and not faint.

Isaiah 40:31 ESV

DEC

NOTES

_____
_____
_____
_____
_____
_____
_____
_____
_____
_____
_____
_____
_____
_____
_____
_____
_____

To Do

- [ ] _____
- [ ] _____
- [ ] _____
- [ ] _____
- [ ] _____
- [ ] _____
- [ ] _____
- [ ] _____
- [ ] _____
- [ ] _____
- [ ] _____
- [ ] _____
- [ ] _____
- [ ] _____
- [ ] _____

DECEMBER

MONDAY 24 Christmas Eve	TUESDAY 25 Christmas Day	WEDNESDAY 26
07:00 AM	07:00 AM	07:00 AM
07:30 AM	07:30 AM	07:30 AM
08:00 AM	08:00 AM	08:00 AM
08:30 AM	08:30 AM	08:30 AM
09:00 AM	09:00 AM	09:00 AM
09:30 AM	09:30 AM	09:30 AM
10:00 AM	10:00 AM	10:00 AM
10:30 AM	10:30 AM	10:30 AM
11:00 AM	11:00 AM	11:00 AM
11:30 AM	11:30 AM	11:30 AM
12:00 PM	12:00 PM	12:00 PM
12:30 PM	12:30 PM	12:30 PM
01:00 PM	01:00 PM	01:00 PM
01:30 PM	01:30 PM	01:30 PM
02:00 PM	02:00 PM	02:00 PM
02:30 PM	02:30 PM	02:30 PM
03:00 PM	03:00 PM	03:00 PM
03:30 PM	03:30 PM	03:30 PM
04:00 PM	04:00 PM	04:00 PM
04:30 PM	04:30 PM	04:30 PM
05:00 PM	05:00 PM	05:00 PM
05:30 PM	05:30 PM	05:30 PM
06:00 PM	06:00 PM	06:00 PM
06:30 PM	06:30 PM	06:30 PM
07:00 PM	07:00 PM	07:00 PM
07:30 PM	07:30 PM	07:30 PM
08:00 PM	08:00 PM	08:00 PM
08:30 PM	08:30 PM	08:30 PM

NOVEMBER 2018
S	M	T	W	T	F	S
				1	2	3
4	5	6	7	8	9	10
11	12	13	14	15	16	17
18	19	20	21	22	23	24
25	26	27	28	29	30	

DECEMBER 2018
S	M	T	W	T	F	S
						1
2	3	4	5	6	7	8
9	10	11	12	13	14	15
16	17	18	19	20	21	22
23	24	25	26	27	28	29
30	31					

JANUARY 2019
S	M	T	W	T	F	S
		1	2	3	4	5
6	7	8	9	10	11	12
13	14	15	16	17	18	19
20	21	22	23	24	25	26
27	28	29	30	31		

DECEMBER

THURSDAY 27

- 07:00 AM
- 07:30 AM
- 08:00 AM
- 08:30 AM
- 09:00 AM
- 09:30 AM
- 10:00 AM
- 10:30 AM
- 11:00 AM
- 11:30 AM
- 12:00 PM
- 12:30 PM
- 01:00 PM
- 01:30 PM
- 02:00 PM
- 02:30 PM
- 03:00 PM
- 03:30 PM
- 04:00 PM
- 04:30 PM
- 05:00 PM
- 05:30 PM
- 06:00 PM
- 06:30 PM
- 07:00 PM
- 07:30 PM
- 08:00 PM
- 08:30 PM

FRIDAY 28

- 07:00 AM
- 07:30 AM
- 08:00 AM
- 08:30 AM
- 09:00 AM
- 09:30 AM
- 10:00 AM
- 10:30 AM
- 11:00 AM
- 11:30 AM
- 12:00 PM
- 12:30 PM
- 01:00 PM
- 01:30 PM
- 02:00 PM
- 02:30 PM
- 03:00 PM
- 03:30 PM
- 04:00 PM
- 04:30 PM
- 05:00 PM
- 05:30 PM
- 06:00 PM
- 06:30 PM
- 07:00 PM
- 07:30 PM
- 08:00 PM
- 08:30 PM

SATURDAY 29

SUNDAY 30

DECEMBER

MONDAY 31 New Year's Eve	TUESDAY 1 New Year's Day	WEDNESDAY 2
07:00 AM	07:00 AM	07:00 AM
07:30 AM	07:30 AM	07:30 AM
08:00 AM	08:00 AM	08:00 AM
08:30 AM	08:30 AM	08:30 AM
09:00 AM	09:00 AM	09:00 AM
09:30 AM	09:30 AM	09:30 AM
10:00 AM	10:00 AM	10:00 AM
10:30 AM	10:30 AM	10:30 AM
11:00 AM	11:00 AM	11:00 AM
11:30 AM	11:30 AM	11:30 AM
12:00 PM	12:00 PM	12:00 PM
12:30 PM	12:30 PM	12:30 PM
01:00 PM	01:00 PM	01:00 PM
01:30 PM	01:30 PM	01:30 PM
02:00 PM	02:00 PM	02:00 PM
02:30 PM	02:30 PM	02:30 PM
03:00 PM	03:00 PM	03:00 PM
03:30 PM	03:30 PM	03:30 PM
04:00 PM	04:00 PM	04:00 PM
04:30 PM	04:30 PM	04:30 PM
05:00 PM	05:00 PM	05:00 PM
05:30 PM	05:30 PM	05:30 PM
06:00 PM	06:00 PM	06:00 PM
06:30 PM	06:30 PM	06:30 PM
07:00 PM	07:00 PM	07:00 PM
07:30 PM	07:30 PM	07:30 PM
08:00 PM	08:00 PM	08:00 PM
08:30 PM	08:30 PM	08:30 PM

NOTES

_____
_____
_____
_____
_____
_____
_____
_____
_____
_____
_____
_____
_____
_____
_____
_____
_____

To Do

- [ ] _____
- [ ] _____
- [ ] _____
- [ ] _____
- [ ] _____
- [ ] _____
- [ ] _____
- [ ] _____
- [ ] _____
- [ ] _____
- [ ] _____
- [ ] _____
- [ ] _____
- [ ] _____

NOTES

To Do

NOTES

_____
_____
_____
_____
_____
_____
_____
_____
_____
_____
_____
_____
_____
_____
_____
_____
_____

To Do

- [ ] _____
- [ ] _____
- [ ] _____
- [ ] _____
- [ ] _____
- [ ] _____
- [ ] _____
- [ ] _____
- [ ] _____
- [ ] _____
- [ ] _____
- [ ] _____
- [ ] _____
- [ ] _____
- [ ] _____

NOTES

To Do